The Source of Life

The Source of Life

*The Holy Spirit and
the Theology of Life*

Jürgen Moltmann

FORTRESS PRESS

THE SOURCE OF LIFE
The Holy Spirit and the Theology of Life

First Fortress Press edition published 1997.

Translated by Margaret Kohl from the German, *Die Quelle des Lebens: Der Heilige Geist und die Theologie des Lebens,* © Chr Kaiser/Götersloher Verlagshaus, 1997.

Library of Congress Cataloging-in-Publication Data

Moltmann, Jürgen.
    [Quelle des Lebens. English]
    The source of life : the Holy Spirit and the theology of life / by Jürgen Moltmann ; translated by Margaret Kohl.
        p.   cm.
    Includes bibliographical references.
    ISBN 0-8006-3099-8
    1. Holy Spirit.   2. Life.   I. Title.
    BT121.2.M6213   1997   97-25134
    231'.3—dc21   CIP

Cover design: Brad Norr Design.
Cover graphic: "Black House" (1984; oil pastel) by Jennifer Bartlett. Bartlett's works create enigmatic imagery, as in her sensuous handling of the surface and the wondrous inner light coming forth from the densely foliated setting. Reproduced with permission of the St. Louis Art Museum.

                                                                    AF 1-3099
03   02   01   3   4   5   6   7   8   9   10   11

Contents

Contents   vii

Foreword

This little book has grown out of lectures which, following my book *The Spirit of Life* (1991, ET 1992) I have given in congregations and at clergy conferences, and to seminars and faculties in many countries. I have tried to say here as directly and immediately as possible what was put forward in my earlier book in the terminology of academic theology. What cannot be said simply does not need to be said at all. I have therefore largely dispensed with citations and references. These may be found in *The Spirit of Life*. But at the end of the present book I have offered some suggestions for further reading. Large-scale theological books have become expensive, at least in Germany. But theology is a task laid on every Christian. I believe in a general theology of all believers, corresponding to their general priesthood. That is the other reason why I am publishing this little book.

I should like to draw attention to some chapters which are new over against *The Spirit of Life*.

I. 'Wrestling with God. A Personal Meditation on Jacob's Struggle at the Brook Jabbok following Genesis 32.25–32.' I gave this on 13 August 1995 in the Bonhoeffer Church, Forest Hill, London, in remembrance of the theological school behind barbed wire at Norton Camp, 1945–1948. It was there that I came to theology.

II. 'The Holy Spirit and the Theology of Life.' This was a Lambeth Palace Lecture, given at King's College, London, in 1996, and at the meeting of clergy and women evangelists of the Yoidoo Full Gospel Church in Seoul, Korea. It was printed in the *Deutsches Pfarrersblatt* 4/1996, and in the

Journal of Pentecostal Theology 6/1996, as well as in Korea.

IV. 'A Meditation on Hope' was delivered on 2 February 1995 at the Patron Day of the Catholic University of Louvain, Belgium. It appeared in *Orientierung* 6/1995.

X. ' "... And Thou Renewest the Face of the Earth" ' was written for the General Assembly of the World Council of Churches in Canberra, and was published in the *Ecumenical Review* 42, 1990.

XI. 'What Are We Doing When We Pray?' has not hitherto been published.

August 1996   Jürgen Moltmann

I

Wrestling with God

A Personal Meditation on Jacob's Struggle at the Brook Jabbok, following Genesis 32.25-32

Jacob wrestles with God at the Jabbok:

> And Jacob was left alone; and a man wrestled with him until the breaking of the day. When the man saw that he did not prevail against Jacob, he touched the hollow of his thigh; and Jacob's thigh was put out of joint as he wrestled with him. Then he said, 'Let me go, for the day is breaking.' But Jacob said, 'I will not let you go unless you bless me.' And he said to him, 'What is your name?' And he said 'Jacob.' Then he said, 'Your name shall no more be called Jacob, but Israel, for you have striven with God and with men, and have prevailed.' Then Jacob asked him, 'Tell me, I pray, your name.' But he said, 'Why is it that you ask my name?' And there he blessed him. So Jacob called the name of the place Peniel, saying, 'For I have seen God face to face and my soul has been healed.' And the sun rose upon him as he passed Penuel, limping because of his thigh.

In the years I spent as a prisoner of war, 1945-48, the biblical story about Jacob's struggle with the angel of the Lord at the Jabbok was for me always the story about God in which I found again my own little human story. We were caught up in the terrors of the end of the war, and in the hopeless misery of a prisoner of war's existence. We wrestled with God in order to survive in the abysses of senselessness and guilt; and we emerged from those years 'limping' indeed, but blessed. The end of the war, when it at last came, found us with deeply wounded souls; but after the years in Norton Camp many of us said: 'My soul has been healed, for I have seen God.' In the labour camps, the night of cold despair fell on us, and in that night we were visited, each in his own way, by tormenting, gnawing thoughts. But when we emerged, we saw 'that the sun had risen'. As a lasting reminder, as it were, each of had somewhere or other 'his lame hip' – the scars of that time in body and soul. That is why I chose this story, so as with it, and hidden in it, to tell our story as I experienced it.

When we lie awake at night and descend into the deep wells of memory, then suddenly everything is present again, although it is all so long ago. It is as if there were no time. The pains and the blessing are still in us, for they go with us wherever we turn. Out of the profusion of the visions which then swim to the surface, let me take a few, so that we can remember together.

1. *The road to misery*

1. *We were the ones who escaped.* We escaped the mass death of the world war. For every one who survived, hundreds died. Why did we survive? Why aren't we dead like the rest? In July 1943 I was an air force auxiliary in a battery in the centre of Hamburg, and barely survived the fire storm which the Royal Air Force's 'Operation Gomorrah' let loose on the eastern part of the city. The friend standing next to me at the firing predictor was torn to pieces by the bomb that left me unscathed. That night I cried out to God for the first time: 'My God, where are you?' And the question 'Why am I not dead too?' has haunted me ever since. Why are you alive? What gives your life meaning? Life is good, but to be a survivor is hard. One has to bear the weight of grief. It was probably in that night that my theology began, for I came from a secular family and knew nothing of faith. The people who escaped probably all saw their survival not just as a gift but as a charge too.

2. *Lost hopes – tormenting memories.* We had escaped

death, but we were prisoners of war. I was first of all in the wretched mass camp 2226 in Zedelgem near Ostend, then in Labour Camp 22 in Kilmarnock in Ayrshire. It was July 1946 before I came to Norton Camp. The end of the war and the summer of 1945 brought cold horror into the camp: all the German cities in ruins; 12 million people fleeing from East Prussia and Silesia. Many people were face to face with nothing, and didn't know where to go. We had escaped but we had lost all hope. Some of us became cynical, some of us fell ill. The thought of there being no way out was like an iron band constricting our hearts. And each of us tried to conceal his stricken heart behind an armour of untouchability.

Lost Hopes: My spiritual nourishment had been Goethe's poems and his *Faust*, which my sister had given me to take with me ('pocket edition for the armed forces'). These poems had awakened the emotions of the boy, but now, when I was shut into a hut with 200 others, they had nothing more to say to me, although I often said them over to myself. I had dreamed of studying mathematics and physics. Einstein and Heisenberg were my heroes. But in that hut my dream fell to pieces: what was the point of it all?

And then those sleepless nights, when I was overwhelmed by the tormenting memories of the tanks that overran us on the fringes of the battle of Arnhem, and woke up soaked with sweat; when the faces of the dead appeared and looked at me with quenched and sightless eyes. It was five years at least before I found some degree of healing for these memories. In that mass camp, where we just sat around and had nothing to do, one was especially at the mercy of those tormenting memories. In those nights one was 'alone' like Jacob and fought with principalities and powers that seemed dark and dangerous. It was only afterwards, and later, that it became clear with whom one had been wrestling.

And then came what was for me the worst of all. In September 1945, in Camp 22 in Scotland, we were confronted with pictures of Belsen and Auschwitz. They were pinned up in one of the huts, without comment. Some people thought it was just propaganda. Others set the piles of bodies which they saw over against Dresden. But slowly and inexorably the truth filtered into our awareness, and we saw ourselves mirrored in the eyes of the Nazi victims. Was this what we had fought for? Had my generation, as the last, been driven to our deaths so that the concentration camp murderers could go on killing, and Hitler could live a few months longer? Some people were so appalled that they didn't want to go back to Germany ever again. Later they stayed on in England. For me, every feeling for Germany, the so-called sacred 'Fatherland', collapsed. It was only when my father's Jewish friend Fritz Valentin returned to Hamburg from his English exile in 1945 (he was president of the provincial court, a convinced Christian, and later founder of the Protestant Academy in Hamburg) that my father in his French captivity and I in England felt in duty bound to return to that country of contradictions, between Goethe's Weimar and Buchenwald. The depression over the wartime destruction and a captivity without any apparent end was exacerbated by a feeling of profound shame at having to share in this disgrace. That was undoubtedly the hardest thing, a stranglehold that choked us.

2. *The undeserved turn of events*

For me, the turn from humiliation to new hope came about through two things, first through the Bible, and then though the encounter with other people.

In the Scottish labour camp, together with some other astonished prisoners, I was for the first time given a Bible by a well-meaning army chaplain. Some of us would rather have had a few cigarettes. I read it without much comprehension, until I stumbled on the psalms of lament. Psalm 39 held me spellbound: 'I was dumb with silence, I held my peace and my sorrow was stirred' (but Luther's German is much stronger – 'I have to eat up my suffering within myself') . . . my lifetime is as nothing in thy sight . . . Hear my prayer, O Lord, and give ear to my cry; hold not thou thy peace at my tears, for I am a stranger with thee, and a sojourner, as all my fathers were . . .' They were the words of my own heart and they called my soul to God. Then I came to the story of the passion, and when I read Jesus's death cry, 'My God, why have you forsaken me?', I knew with certainty: this is someone who understands you. I began to understand the assailed Christ because I felt that he understood me: this was the divine brother in distress, who takes the prisoners with him on his way to resurrection. I began to summon up the courage to live again, seized by a great hope. I was even calm when other men were 'repatriated' and I was not. This early fellowship with Jesus, the brother in suffering and the redeemer from guilt, has never left me since. I never 'decided for Christ' as is often demanded of us, but I am sure that then and there, in the dark pit of my soul, he found me. Christ's God-forsakenness showed me *where* God is, *where* he had been with me in my life, and where he would be in the future.

The other thing was the kindness with which Scots and English, our former enemies, came to meet us half way. In Kilmarnock the miners and their families took us in with a hospitality which shamed us profoundly. We heard no reproaches, we were accused of no guilt. We were accepted as people, even though we were just numbers and wore our prisoners' patches on our backs. We experienced forgiveness of guilt without any confession of guilt on our part, and that made it possible for us to live with the past of our people, and in the shadow of Auschwitz, without repressing anything, and without becoming callous. I corresponded with the Steele family for a long time afterwards.

The other experience which turned my life upside down was the first international SCM conference at Swanwick, in the summer of 1947, to which a group of PoWs was invited. We came there still wearing our wartime uniforms. And we came with fear and trembling. What were we to say about the war crimes, and the mass murders in the concentration camps? But we were welcomed as brothers in Christ, and were able to eat and drink, pray and sing with young Christians who had come from all over the world, even from

Australia and New Zealand. In the night my eyes sometimes filled with tears.

Then a group of Dutch students came and asked to speak to us officially. Again I was frightened, for I had fought in Holland, in the battle for the Arnhem bridge. The Dutch students told us that Christ was the bridge on which they could cross to us, and that without Christ they would not be talking to us at all. They told of the Gestapo terror, the loss of their Jewish friends, and the destruction of their homes. We too could step on to this bridge which Christ had built from them to us, and could confess the guilt of our people and ask for reconciliation. At the end we all embraced. For me that was an hour of liberation. I was able to breathe again, felt like a human being once more, and returned cheerfully to the camp behind the barbed wire. The question of how long the captivity was going to last no longer bothered me.

In some English circles, Norton Camp counted as a camp where young Germans were supposed to be 're-educated' for a better Germany. But in reality it was a generous gift of reconciliation offered to former enemies; and as such it was unique. I came to the camp in the autumn of 1946. My wartime Abitur – the school leaving certificate – was no longer accepted and I had to go back to school. The decision whether I should become a teacher and pastor was made for me through my experiences with the Bible and at the Swanwick conference. In the evenings I often walked along the camp fence and looked up at the chapel on the hill: 'I circle round God, the age-old tower . . .' I was still searching, but I sensed that God was drawing me, and that I should not be seeking him if he had not already found me. On 15 August 1946, I wrote to my family: 'I end most days in a curious way. In our camp there is a hill, overgrown with huge old trees. It is really the centre of camp life, for there is a little chapel on it where we meet for evening prayers, so as to end the day with a hymn and collect our thoughts for new life. I like to sit there in the evening and look through the "Norman" windows into the twilight, out on to the lake and the fields. Perhaps we ought to see this whole imprisonment as a great church-going . . .' We loved the chapel. It cast a wholly unique spell over us.

3. The blessing of Norton Camp

For us, Norton Camp was a kind of monastic enclosure, 'excluded from time and world', as Gerhard Noller wrote in 1948 in his farewell letter. The day began at 6.30 with a bugle call (because we had lost our watches when we were taken prisoner) and ended at 10.30 p.m., when the English put out the lights. All at once we had time, time in plenty, and stood, spiritually and mentally starving as we were, in front of a wonderful library put together by the YMCA. During those days I read everything – poems and novels, mathematics and philosophy, as well as any amount of theology – and that literally from morning to night. Everything, and the theology especially, was fabulously new to me. The YMCA also printed books for the help of PoWs. I still have some of them – Nygren's *Eros und Agape* and Bonhoeffer's *Nachfolge* (*The Cost of Discipleship*). My first book of systematic theology was Reinhold Niebuhr's *The Nature and Destiny of Man*, which made a deep impression on me, although I hardly understood it. New worlds dawned for us, worlds which had been forbidden to us under the Third Reich. We read émigré literature, as well as the work of modern English and American writers.

The semester timetables were rich and varied, and of course we wanted to hear everything. I learnt Hebrew under Walter Haaren and Gerhard Noller. Gerhard Friedrich introduced us to the New Testament. And then there were the visitors from outside: Anders Nygren stayed a fortnight and taught us systematic theology. Professor Søe from Copenhagen did the same for Christian ethics. Werner Milch, an emigrant, later in Marburg, enthralled us with a history of twentieth-century literature. Fritz Blanke came from Zürich, and Matthew Black from Scotland. I met him again later in St Andrews. Of course we were a 'show camp', and not with-

out reason; but we were also richly benefited and honoured
by the visits and addresses of Birger Forell, John Mott,
Willem Visser't Hooft, Martin Niemöller and others.

I think not least of the moving sermons by our camp
chaplains Rudolf Halver and Wilhelm Burckert. They were
the first sermons I had ever heard, and I could still repeat
some of them today, especially Halver's sermon of 10 August
1947, on the *magna peccatrix*, the woman who was a great
sinner. I can still see in my mind's eye the long procession of
prisoners on their way to Cuckney church, or to the
Methodist church where Frank Baker was minister. I met
him again later at Duke University in Durham, USA.

At night we sometimes crawled through a hole at the right
hand corner of the back fence so as to fetch wood from the
Duke of Portland's park for the iron stove that stood in the
middle of the hut. How much time we had for night-time
talks in the firelight of the stove, long after the lights had
been put out! Never again have I lived 'the life of the mind'
as intensively as I did in the last semester of the theological
school in Norton camp. It was a marvellous, a richly blessed
time. We were given what we did not deserve, and received
of the fullness of Christ 'grace upon grace'.

4. *Limping but blessed*

For us, what looked like a grim fate when it began turned
into an undeserved, rich blessing. It began in the night of
war, and when we came to Norton Camp the sun rose for us.
We came with wounded souls, and when we left 'my soul
was healed'. Certainly we did not 'see God face to face' like
Jacob at that place on the Jabbok. According to biblical
tradition, that is reserved for only a few 'friends of God'; for
all others it is promised only for the great day of resurrection,
when we shall see 'face to face' and 'know as we are known'.
No, what we experienced was just the reverse: God looked
on us with 'the shining eyes' of his eternal joy. Blessing and
the Spirit of life always have their origin in 'the light of God's
countenance' (Pss. 51.11; 139.7; Num. 6.24–26), just as his

judgment means his 'hidden face' (*hester panim*), and rejection is the face of God when it is 'turned away'. What we
experienced was for many of us the turn from God's 'hidden
face' to 'the light of his countenance'. We experienced with
pain his hiddenness and remoteness, and we sensed that he
looked upon us 'with shining eyes', and felt the warmth of
his great love.

We have met together here after fifty years in order to
praise the hidden and yet so merciful God for everything
which we have experienced of him. We have also come to
remember with gratitude the people who came to meet us
prisoners with such readiness to forgive, and such hospitality. We shall never forget Birger Forell and John Barwick,
who set up Norton Camp, and we have lasting ties with the
YMCA, which organized that generous 'prisoners' aid'
which raised us up. Let me close with Psalm 30, verse 11, and
acknowledge:

> Lord, thou hast turned for me my mourning into dancing;
> Thou hast loosed my sackcloth and girded me with glad-
> ness,
> that my soul may praise thee and not be silent.
> O Lord my God, I will give thanks to thee for ever.

II

The Holy Spirit and the Theology of Life

The gift and the presence of the Holy Spirit is the greatest and most wonderful thing which we can experience – we ourselves, the human community, all living things and this earth. For with the Holy Spirit it is not just one random spirit that is present, among all the many good and evil spirits that there are. It is *God himself*, the creative and life-giving, redeeming and saving God. Where the Holy Spirit is present, God is present in a special way, and we experience God through our lives, which become wholly living from within. We experience whole, full, healed and redeemed life, experience it with all our senses. We feel and taste, we touch and see our life in God and God in our life. There are many names for God the Holy Spirit, but of them all the Comforter (Paraclete) and the well of life (*fons vitae*) are the names I like best.

1. *The presence of God's Spirit: biblical perspectives*

The expectation and coming of the Holy Spirit

Prayers to the Holy Spirit are all fundamentally a plea for *the Spirit's coming*. That is something special. Christian tradition calls it the *epiklesis of the Spirit*. Most Pentecostal hymns simply cry 'Come, Creator Spirit' (we may think of Rabanus Maurus's '*Veni, Creator Spiritus*'). The prayer for the Holy Spirit is a plea for the Spirit's all-embracing presence. The Spirit is more than just one of God's gifts among others; the Holy Spirit is the unrestricted presence of

God in which our life wakes up, becomes wholly and entirely living, and is endowed with the energies of life. Prayers for the coming of the Holy Spirit are *maranatha* prayers. As we all know, *maranatha* prayers are addressed to Christ and are meant eschatologically:

'Amen. Yes, come Lord Jesus' is the penultimate saying in the New Testament (Rev. 22.20). Here too it is not just the person of Jesus that is meant; it is his coming in the glory of God for the new creation of the world. The parousia of the Holy Spirit is nothing other than the beginning of the parousia of Christ. That is why the Holy Spirit is called the pledge or down-payment of glory (Eph. 1.14; II Cor. 1.22). So what begins in the Holy Spirit *here* will be completed and perfected in the kingdom of glory *there*. The kingdom of glory does not come unexpectedly and without any preparation. It is already heralded in the kingdom of the Spirit, where it already has power in the present. The relation is like the relation between spring and summer, seedtime and harvest, sunrise and high noon.

In the plea for the coming of the Spirit, the people who cry out for its coming open themselves for what they expect, and let the energies of the Spirit stream into their lives. Even if people can do no more than sigh for redemption, and then fall dumb even as they sigh, God's Spirit already sighs within them and intercedes for them (Rom. 8.26). The pleading and the sighing for the coming of God into this imprisoned life and into this disrupted world themselves come from the Holy Spirit, and are the first signs of the Spirit's life.

We continually experience the Holy Spirit as both a divine counterpart *to whom* we call, and a divine presence *in which* we call – as the space we live in. There is nothing extraordinary about this. As children we experienced our mothers as both too – as a presence surrounding us and a counterpart calling us.

The response to the plea for the Holy Spirit is the Spirit's coming and remaining, its outpouring and its indwelling. People who ask for the Holy Spirit to come to us – into our hearts, into the community we live in, and to our earth –

don't want to flee into heaven or to be snatched away into the next world. They have hope for their hearts, their community and this earth. We don't pray 'Let us come into your kingdom' either. We pray 'Your kingdom come *on earth as in heaven.*' The petition for the coming of the divine Spirit to us frail earthly people implies a great, unbroken affirmation of life.

Another response to the petition for the Holy Spirit is its 'outpouring on all flesh' (Joel 2.28; Acts 2.17ff.). This is a quite astounding metaphor. What is it saying? 'All flesh' is of course human life first and foremost but, as Gen. 9.10ff. says, it also embraces all the living generally – plants, trees and animals. In Ps. 36.9 God himself is called 'the well of life'. In John 4.14 Jesus tells the Samaritan woman that he will give the 'water' which wells up out of the fountain of eternal life. The image of 'the wellspring of life', and the water which gives life to everything that is parched and dried up, is used as a way of explaining the effect of the Holy Spirit. As 'the water of life', the Spirit makes what is dying and withered living and fertile.

The astonishing thing is that here the Holy Spirit is seen not just as a divine Person but as *the divine element* too. The Spirit is 'sent' and 'comes' like a tempest; it spreads itself out over all living things, like the waters of a flood, pervading everything. If the Holy Spirit is God's Spirit and the special presence of God, then when God's Spirit is poured out, 'all flesh' will be deified. All mortal flesh will be filled with the eternal life of God, for what comes from God is divine and eternal like God himself. In 'the outpouring of God's Spirit', God opens himself and becomes what the the mystic and poet Mechthild of Magdeburg calls 'the outpouring and flowing Godhead'. In the source, the river and the lake, the quality of the water is the same, but its flow is graduated. The transition from the Spirit itself to the Spirit's many different energies – from the charis to the charismata – is as fluid as an emanation. The divine becomes the all-embracing presence in which what is human – indeed everything that lives – can develop fruitfully and live eternally: 'You encompass me on every side and hold your hand over me' (Ps. 139.5).

The origin and communication of the Holy Spirit

The question about the origin of the Holy Spirit is not a speculative question. It is a necessary one; for in the origin the goal is already inherent. The Holy Spirit brings and communicates that from which it originates or springs. So what is this? From what does the Holy Spirit originate?

The shining face of God

The answer the Old Testament gives us is a surprising one: 'Cast me not away from thy presence and take not thy holy Spirit from me', we pray with Ps. 51.11 (cf. also Ps. 139.7). And with Ps. 104.29ff. we recognize that it can be said of every living thing that 'When thou hidest thy face, they are dismayed; when thou takest away thy breath (Spirit) they die, and return to dust. Thou sendest forth thy breath (Spirit) and they are created, and thou renewest the face of the earth.'

'The face of God' is a symbol for God's commitment, the attention with which he looks at us, and his special presence. It is always the face that reveals the inward play of the emotions. Our irritation and our joy, our laughing and our weeping show in our faces; and the same is true in a trans-ferred sense about the face of God. In Jewish thinking God's 'hidden face' is a symbol of God's judgment. For God's face to be turned away is a symbol of God's rejection and of eternal death. But God's 'shining countenance' is the source of the outpouring of the Spirit and of God's life, love and blessing. 'Make your face shine upon us and be gracious,' we pray in the Aaronitic blessing. That is the prayer for the Holy Spirit, the special, life-giving presence of God among us.

When does someone's face shine? People's faces begin to shine in the look of love. When a mother takes her child in her arms and loves it, we see her eyes shining. When some-

one wants to give someone else a wonderful gift, the giver's
eyes light up in expectant excitement. Radiant eyes bring
joy. In terms of physics, the eyes merely absorb light, but
physiognomically the soul 'radiates' from them. We can
imagine all this and more when we think of God's 'shining
face' and await the light of the Holy Spirit from that source.
Assurance of life and new energies for living awaken in us
when God looks at us with the shining eyes of his joy.
According to Luke 15, human repentance gives God the joy
that we feel when we find something we had lost. The face of
God, shining for joy, is the luminous source of the Holy
Spirit. The light floods over us, and our faces become mirrors
which reflect that light and diffuse it.

According to Paul, the glory of God shines 'in the face of
Jesus Christ' and casts 'a bright shining into our hearts' (II
Cor. 4.6). Then we too will reflect the glory of the Lord 'with
unveiled face' (II Cor. 3.18). Our 'hidden' faces keep us from
knowing ourselves and hide us from ourselves. Our longing
for self-encounter and self-experience comes from this
hiddenness and will be satisfied only in that apocalypse when
God is seen 'face to face' (I Cor. 13.12). Experience of the
Spirit is the 'bright shining in our hearts' which begins the
apocalypse of ourselves.

Earlier generations liked to depict the illuminating power
or radiance of the saints as their haloes, or as the golden
background to icons. Every human life and every human face
radiates its own atmosphere. Trust and mistrust, tranquillity
and bustle, peace and anxiety radiate from us and communi-
cate themselves to other people. Every aura is the outcome of
what we most of all fear and most of all love. It can be our
own ego, but it can also be God. We are unconscious of the
divine radiance, inevitably so, because 'the person who looks
at himself does not shine', as Lao Tsu rightly says. But if
people look away from themselves to Christ – from these
people the spirit of Christ begins to shine.

The goal of Christ's self-giving and his resurrection

In the New Testament the Holy Spirit issues from the events of Christ's history, which are events in salvation history. It is these that we celebrate in the church's year too: Christmas – Good Friday – Easter – Ascension Day – Pentecost. Pentecost is the final festival in this sequence, so it is also the goal towards which the other feasts point.

We can see at a glance that the history of Christ and the history of the Holy Spirit are dovetailed and indissolubly intertwined: according to the Synoptic Gospels Christ comes from the Holy Spirit – 'conceived by the Holy Spirit', baptized by the Holy Spirit – performs miracles and proclaims the kingdom of God in the power of the Spirit, surrenders himself to his redeeming death on the cross through the eternal Spirit, is raised by God through the life-giving Spirit, and in the Spirit is present among us now. *Christ's history in the Spirit* begins with his baptism and ends in his resurrection. Then things are reversed. Christ sends the Spirit upon the community of his people and is present in the Spirit. That is *the history of the Spirit in Christ*. The Spirit of God becomes the Spirit of Christ. The Christ sent in the Spirit becomes Christ the sender of the Spirit.

If we look closer still, we come face to face with the mystery of Christ's death and life, and discover that it is out of this mystery of Christ that the Spirit of life springs. Luke certainly tells the mystery as a sequence of events in salvation history, with time intervals which are meant symbolically: after 'three days' rose again from the dead – after 'forty days' ascended into heaven – after 'fifty days' the outpouring of the Spirit on the assembled community. But in actual fact this is one single event, the event of the coming of God for the salvation of the world.

We can make this clear to ourselves if we look more closely at the Easter faith of Jesus's men and women disciples. Jesus was crucified publicly. His resurrection from the dead was experienced only by the women in Jerusalem and the disciples in Galilee, to whom he himself appeared as the risen Christ. This experience transformed them utterly.

The disciples returned to Jerusalem, although they must have expected to meet the same death there as Christ himself. They had found a faith that overcomes the world and were not afraid of anything any more. The men and women who 'saw' the risen Christ because he 'appeared' to them personally, also received the Spirit of the resurrection, as John 20.22 stresses: 'Receive the Holy Spirit', says the risen Christ. So the appearance of the risen Christ and the outpouring of the Holy Spirit – Easter faith and Pentecostal experience – belong together in a single whole, and are not differentiated in time. To recognize the risen Christ and to experience the energies of our own rebirth in the Spirit of the resurrection are one. If this were not so, there would be faith in a dead Christ, and a spiritual rebirth without Christ. We can also make this clear to ourselves if we remember that the people who for forty days lived in the visible presence of the risen Christ did not found a religion of divine visions. When the appearances of the risen Christ came to an end, these people went on living in faith: 'Blessed are those who have not seen and yet believe' (John 20.29). The presence of Christ in appearances became the presence of Christ in the Spirit, because in Christ's appearances the Spirit was already present.

True Easter faith is the work of the Spirit, for believing in Christ's resurrection doesn't mean affirming a historical fact, and saying 'Oh really?' It means being seized by the life-giving Spirit and experiencing 'the powers of the world to come' (Heb. 6.5) in our own living and dying. There is no Pentecost without Easter. That is obvious. But there is no Easter without Pentecost either. There is no Easter theology without a theology of Pentecost, and no Pentecost theology without Easter theology.

The crucified Christ and the sending of the Spirit by the Father

What I have described up to now was the external, historical side of salvation, so to speak. But there is a divine, inward side as well. John 14 probes this comprehensively. The chapter is part of Jesus's 'farewell discourses', where his 'farewell' means his dying for the redemption of the world, and the redemption of the world is linked with the coming of 'the Paraclete', as the Holy Spirit is called here: 'If I do not go away, the Counsellor will not come to you; but if I go, I will send him to you' (16.7). Here the new beginning of life in the Holy Spirit is directly linked with the mystery of redemption. Through the force of his surrender of himself to death on the cross, Christ sends the Spirit of life. That is the revelation of love in the pain of God, which makes new life for sinners and the dying possible. The papal encyclical *Dominum et vivificantem* of 1986 brings out this inward connection between Good Friday and Pentecost very well. A true theology of the cross is Pentecost theology, and Christian Pentecost theology is a theology of the cross.

If we look back to John 14, the connection is somewhat more complex, because it is a trinitarian connection. According to John 14.16, Jesus goes away so that he may 'pray the Father that he will give you another Comforter'. According to John 14.26, Christ 'sends' this Comforter 'from the Father'. It is 'the Spirit of truth, who proceeds from the Father'. According to this idea, the Holy Spirit is beside the Father of Jesus Christ, and Christ 'goes away' – that is to say he dies – in order to ask the Father to send the Spirit, and in order to send the Spirit from the Father. So the Holy Spirit 'proceeds' from the Father and is sent by the Son. Between Christ the recipient of the Spirit and Christ the sender of the Spirit stands God the Father, as the Holy Spirit's eternal origin. The Holy Spirit does not 'proceed from the Father and the Son', as the Western church's Nicene Creed maintains. The Spirit proceeds from the Father, rests on the Son, and from the Son radiates into the world.

People often ask about a criterion for 'testing' or distinguishing the spirits. For the community of Christ's people this criterion is *the name of Jesus* and *the sign of the cross*. By calling on the name of Jesus, and with the sign of the cross, the evil spirits are banished and God's good Spirit is summoned. So what is true in the negative sense for exorcism is true positively for recognition of the Holy Spirit. What can endure in the face of the crucified Christ is from God; what cannot endure is not from God. The spirit of violence, of greedy possession and arrogance cannot endure. The spirit of love, sharing and humility can endure. It is always the sign of the cross which makes it necessary to distinguish between the spirits. With the name of Jesus the way of Jesus Christ is invoked as well. What serves *the discipleship of Jesus*, and can be put to use there, comes from the Holy Spirit, and what comes from the Holy Spirit leads us along the way of Jesus Christ and into his discipleship. What the Synoptic Gospels call the discipleship of Jesus, the apostle Paul calls life in the Spirit. So personal and public, political and economic discipleship of Jesus is the practical criterion for 'testing the spirits'.

2. *The mission of the Holy Spirit today*

During the last five years a 'theology of life' has emerged all over the world which gives reason for new ecumenical hopes. Most recently Pope John Paul II issued the encyclical *Evangelium vitae* (30 March 1995), in which he contrasted 'the culture of life' with a modern 'culture of death'. In Larnaca in 1993 the Commission of Unity III of the World Council of Churches resolved to initiate a study programme on 'the theology of life'. At the General Assembly of the WCC in Canberra in 1991 the Korean Chung Hyung Kyung invoked a culture of solidarity based on 'the culture of life'. In 1984 Gustavo Gutiérrez's book *The God of Life* appeared (ET 1991), in 1991 my own *The Spirit of Life* (ET 1992), in 1992 Michael Welker's *God the Spirit* (ET 1994), and in 1993 Geiko Müller-Fahrenholz's *God's Spirit Transforms a World in Crisis* (ET 1995). Whereas John Paul II concentrates on unborn life, Gutiérrez turns his eyes towards life that is starving and sick. Whereas the Geneva (WCC) publications draw together perspectives for creation, peace and liberation theology, I myself was concerned about the apathetic, meaningless life of people in the Western world. The theological approach by way of the experience of Pentecost ought to make an integral theology of life possible.

The mission of life

In its original and eternal sense, mission is God's mission (*missio Dei*). It is only when our Christian mission follows the divine sending and corresponds to it that it is a mission with confidence in God and an assured faith. It is only when we as people follow God's mission to other people and put ourselves in line with that mission that we show respect for the dignity of others, as people created by God and made in his image; and it is only then that we shall resist the temptation to try to dominate them religiously.

God's mission is nothing less than the sending of the Holy Spirit from the Father through the Son into this world, so that this world should not perish but live. The Gospel of John tells us quite simply what it is that is brought into the world from God through Christ: *life*. 'I live, and you shall live also' (John 14.19). For the Holy Spirit is 'the source of life' and brings life into the world – whole life, full life, unhindered, indestructible, *everlasting* life. The creative and life-giving Spirit of God already brings this eternally living life here and now, before death, not just after death, because the Spirit brings Christ into this world and Christ is 'the resurrection and the life' in person. With Christ, 'indestructible life' has come to light, and the life spirit which Christ sends into the world is the power of the resurrection, which brings us new life. The sending of the Holy Spirit is the revelation of God's indestructible *affirmation* of life and his marvellous *joy* in life. Where Jesus is, there is life. That is what the Synoptic Gospels tell us. Where Jesus is, sick people are healed, sad people are comforted, marginalized people are accepted, and the demons of death are driven out. Where the Holy Spirit is present there is life. That is what the Acts of the Apostles and the apostolic letters tell us; for where the Spirit is, there is joy at the victory of life over death, and there the powers and energies of eternal life are experienced. So in this divine sense mission is simply and solely a movement for life and a movement of healing, which spreads consolation and the courage to live, and raises up what wants to die. Jesus didn't bring a new religion into the world. What he brought was new life. What does this mean for our understanding of Christian mission?

Up to now mission as we know it has meant the spread of the Christian *imperium*, Christian civilization, or the religious values of the Western world. Up to now mission as we know it has meant the spread and propagation of the church that guarantees eternal salvation. Up to now mission as we know it has been the communication of the personal decision of faith and personal experiences of conversion. But is citizenship of the Christian *imperium* or Christian civilization or the community of Western values already the new life in God's Spirit? Is membership of the Christian church already salvation in the Holy Spirit? Is the experience of conversion and the decision of faith already rebirth out of God's eternal Spirit?

In those traditional forms of Christian mission the terms in which we saw the sending of the Spirit and the new life were evidently too narrow. Of course a Christian life style, the community of the church, and the decisions and experiences of personal faith are all part of it. But the mission of the Holy Spirit is the mission of new life, and that is something more. We must find ways that lead 'from religion to the kingdom of God, from the church to the world, from concern about our own selves to hope for the whole', wrote Christoph Blumhardt, the Württemberg revivalist preacher a hundred years ago.

For us today that means that instead of spreading a Christian civilization or the values of the Western world we have to build up a universal 'culture of life' and resist 'the barbarism of death' wherever we are, as Pope John II put it in his recent public declarations. In our Western European and American countries the affirmation of life has become the main problem. We have long since lost the hybris of earlier world conquerors. Our feeling about life has become *tristesse*. We seem to be paralysed by a chilly apathy. Our social coldness towards the poor and strangers shows that we have no love for their lives. We see the misery in Bosnia and Rwanda on the TV screen, but it no longer touches us. Knowledge doesn't mean power any longer. Knowledge means powerlessness: 'after all, there's nothing we can do about it' – so we hold our tongues and stay mute. Humanity is likely to die of apathy of soul like this before it founders in social or military catastrophes. We need nothing so much as *the mission of life* so that we can again affirm and love life so much that we protest against death and all the powers that disseminate death. What we need is not a new religion, or new peace between the religions. What we need is life – whole, full, and undivided life. Isn't this the essence of the gospel: God, the eternal, infinite God, is so close to you that he loves you, and in his love accepts you just as you are? People who feel the faintest spark of this love become conscious of their own dignity, get up and walk upright and live with heads held high. Even when we are loved by another person, our energy for living awakens, and we trust ourselves to do more than we would ever have dared before. How much more is this the case when God looks at us with the 'shining eyes' of his love and his pleasure in our lives! That is why part of this message of life is the comforting of the sad, the healing of the sick – the healing, too, of memories –, the welcoming of strangers and the forgiving of sins. That is to say, the message of life means saving threatened and impaired life from the powers of annihilation.

But for us this also means that in place of the spread of our Orthodox, Roman Catholic or Protestant churches we have to put a passion for the kingdom of God. Mission doesn't mean 'compelling them to come in'! It is the *invitation* to God's future and to hope for the new creation of all things: 'Behold, I am making all things new' – and you are invited to this divine future for the world! In God's Spirit you can already anticipate now this becoming-new which God will complete on his day. Once a passion for God's future replaces a passion for the spread of the church we shall stop exporting our ugly European and American church divisions, and extending religious denominationalism instead of hope for the kingdom of God. In China, after the anti-religious cultural revolution, when Christians emerged again from the camps and the underground into public life, there were no longer Methodists, Baptists, Episcopalians and Presbyterians. Now there were only members of the one church of Christ, and it spread so rapidly that every day a new church was opened, so that today between forty and sixty million people belong. Probably the experience of shared persecution and martyrs is always needed before the divided churches can arrive at ecumenical fellowship, and subordinate their own interests to the kingdom of God which is common to them all. The mission to the churches goes ahead of the churches' mission to the world, and today it says: 'Seek first the kingdom of God and his righteousness'; then the living community of God's Spirit will fall to your lot simply of itself.

This mission of life doesn't come without premises; it picks up the thread wherever life exists, wherever life is threatened by violence and death, wherever life withers because the courage for living has been lost. The eternal life of God's Spirit is not a different life from this life here; it is the power that makes this life here different. '*This* perishable nature must put on the imperishable and *this* mortal nature must put on immortality', stresses Paul (I Cor. 15.53). The Holy Spirit's wave of salvation embraces the whole of life and everything living, and cannot be confined to religion and spirituality.

Experience of the Spirit in the context of the new creation of all things

We shall now follow the mission of the Holy Spirit in three waves, asking what happens there, and how we can participate in it.

The renewal of God's people. The first Christian Pentecostal community (Acts 2.17ff.) understood what happened to it as being the fulfilment of Joel's prophecy (Joel 2.28–32). In the End-time, with its terrible catastrophes, God's Spirit will be 'poured out on all flesh'. Of course this initially means all human life, as the next sentence makes plain. But it is not just the devout 'flesh' of Israel which is meant but *all* flesh, the whole of humanity. By the word 'flesh' Joel means especially 'the weak, the people without power and without hope', says H.W. Wolff. 'Your sons and your daughters shall prophesy, your old men shall dream dreams.' The young people who have not yet fully entered into life and the old people who no longer participate in life in all its fullness will experience this Spirit of life first. Those who are still too young or already too old receive the outpouring of the Spirit. This brings about a new equality between the generations: no one is too young, no one is too old, all are equal in their reception of the new life spirit. Youth is no advantage and age is no disadvantage. 'Sons and daughters' will prophesy, 'menservants and maidservants' receive the Spirit. Men and women are put on the same level. Women are just as close to God's Spirit as men. There is no longer any male prerogative. In the Holy Spirit a new messianic community of women and men prophesies, men and women equally endowed and with equal rights. Consequently from the very beginning – and about this there is no dispute – the first Christian community baptized men and women alike, thus recognizing them as endowed with the Spirit. Does a Christian church which only ordains men and excludes women from the proclamation – prophecy – have the Holy Spirit? Or is it 'quenching' the Spirit and repressing its liberating activity?

In the experience of the Spirit a new community of rich and poor, the educated and the uneducated comes into being. The Spirit of God is no respecter of social distinctions; it puts an end to them. All Spirit-impelled revival movements in the history of Christianity have taken note of these socially revolutionary elements in the experience of the Spirit and have spread them. They became a danger to the patriarchy, the men's church and the slave-owners. Today these experiences of the Spirit among children and old people is a danger for those who are pushing the very young and the old on to the fringes of life.

If the Spirit of life descends on vulnerable and mortal life, then it descends on everything living which is threatened by the great cosmic catastrophes – 'the sun shall be turned to darkness, and the moon to blood'. Ultimately the ruling classes belong here too, the rich and 'the beautiful people' who grab life for themselves. Simply by existing, the Spirit-filled community of old and young, men and women, masters and servants, proclaims and testifies to the world 'salvation in danger', the things that endure in a world that passes away, and therefore eternal future in transitory time.

The renewal of all the living. According to the Old Testament, spirit (*ruach*) is *the breath of God's life*. God creates everything through his Spirit. If he withdraws the breath of his life, everything disintegrates into dust (Ps. 104.29ff.). In this cosmic context 'all things' means 'all flesh'. Job 34.14: 'If God should take back his spirit to himself, and gather to himself his breath, all flesh would perish together and human beings would return to dust.' It is this breath of God's life which 'fills the world and holds together all things' (Wisdom 1.7; Isa. 34.16). All things are called into being out of God's living breath, and that breath 'holds them together' in a community of creation which furthers life. If they cut themselves off from that community, they lose the living Spirit. If they destroy the community, they destroy themselves. The Spirit of life means especially the connections and cohesions of everything created, as Michael Welker points out. All things are mutually dependent; they live with each other and for each other, and often enough symbiotically within each other. Life is community, and community is the communication of life.

Like the Spirit of creation, the Spirit of the new creation creates communities for living shared by human beings and other living things, just as it creates communities among people. The new creation doesn't abolish bodiliness. It renews it for eternal livingness. People lose their 'hearts of stone' and acquire 'hearts of flesh' when God puts his Spirit of life into their innermost selves (Ezek. 11.19; 36.27). Shalom will bring human beings and animals into a new shared life, as Isaiah 11 prophesies. When 'the Spirit is poured upon us from on high, and the wilderness becomes a fruitful field, and the fruitful field is deemed a forest, then justice will dwell in the wilderness, and righteousness abide in the fruitful field' (Isa 32.15f.). This can be called the ecology of God's Spirit.

'And thou renewest the face of the earth.' Like all the living things with which we live, people are created out of the earth (Genesis 2). This earth is our shared environment and in a realistic sense 'our mother' (Ecclus. 40.1). By the earth we don't just mean the ground *on* which we stand; we mean the global system with its atmosphere and biosphere *in* which we live. According to biblical traditions, it is the earth that 'brings forth' plants, trees and animals, and human beings are taken from her too. This living-space earth is part of the community of creation shared by all the living. It was modern industrial society which for the first time viewed the earth simply as matter, and no longer as holy. It is time for us to respect the *holiness* of God's earth once more, before the catastrophes descend on us. God's Spirit fills 'the world', as Israel's Wisdom says. The kingdom of God, whose beginning and seal here and today is the Holy Spirit, will bring 'a new heaven and a new earth' (Revelation 21). There is no eternal life without the kingdom of God, and no kingdom of God without the new earth.

III

Born Again to a Living Hope

1. *New life begins in the Spirit*

From early on, Christians associated the beginning of their experience of God in the community of Christ with an overwhelming new experience of their own selves. They didn't just *feel* 'new born', as we say when we have recovered from a serious illness. They *were* 'new born' out of the Spirit which had laid hold of them. Christian faith isn't just a conviction, a feeling and a decision. It invades life so deeply that we have to talk about dying and being born again, which is what corresponds to the death and resurrection of Christ. In the Pentecostal churches, Christians call themselves 'born again' if they have experienced a profound and lasting endowment with the Spirit in their lives. But in the earliest days of Christianity, faith itself was already sealed by baptism, and it was by baptism that it was represented. In the water of baptism, the believer dies to the laws and requirements of 'this world' and is born into the new life with Christ in the Holy Spirit. That is why our Christian name is our baptismal name. It is a way of pointing to a person's new identity, the identity of his or her new life. But when infant baptism was introduced, the 'first' name given at birth and the baptismal name were made to coincide, so that it was no longer possible to distinguish between birth into this mortal life and new birth into the life that is eternal. It is only in later experiences of life and death that we can come to discern the difference, and experience the powers and energies of the new birth in faith. But this does not mean that people should be 're-baptized', for then there would in principle

have to be more than one 're-baptism', to match corresponding experiences of the Spirit. The 'one baptism', however, would be clear to people. They could link their new
experiences of the Spirit with the baptism they had received,
and could make or renew their baptismal vow in freedom.

There is no need for us to go into the problems of infant
baptism and re-baptism here. What we are concerned with at
this point are the facts. And they are exciting enough: the
experience of the Spirit leads to such a new experience of the
self that we have to talk about the birth of a new life. But if
we talk about a new birth out of the Spirit, we then have to
call the Holy Spirit of God 'the mother of believers', and
talk about the Spirit as our divine mother. Otherwise the
metaphor 'birth from the Spirit' (John 3.3–6) would be
meaningless. But the femininity or motherliness of the Holy
Spirit has consequences for the community of women and
men. It makes this community of sisters and brothers a community of free and equal people.

Some people call this experience rebirth. But that is really
wrong, because it leads to the error of reincarnation. The
Greek word *palingenesia* is taken from oriental cosmology
and was introduced into the ancient world by the
Pythagoreans. It means the rebirth of the times of this world.
The eras of world time are caught up in the cycle of eternal
return. The festival of the New Year celebrates the year's
rebirth. And every Sunday proclaims the rebirth of the week.
With the passing of time the world grows old, so if life is to
go on, the world has continually to be born again out of its
eternal origin. The Indian doctrine of reincarnation maintains that human life too is born and dies and is 'born again'
in other forms of life, until one day the soul is released from
the wheel of rebirth and can enter into Nirvana. One New
Testament passage, Matt. 19.28, talks about 'the rebirth of
the cosmos'. When the cosmos is reborn, the Son of man will
sit upon the throne of glory and will judge the world. Here
the doctrine of the unending rebirths of the cosmos is turned
into something final and once-and-for-all, in an apocalyptic
sense. The judgment of the Son of Man will be followed by

the kingdom of glory, which is eternal and never grows old.

When we use the word 'new' we sometimes simply mean 'again' – for example when we say that something has continually to be begun *anew*. But that is not what the New Testament means. In the New Testament, whatever is called 'new' is unique and eternal and never returns again. The person who is 'born anew', as John 3.3 puts it, sees the eternal kingdom of God, the ultimate and eternal future of the passing time of this world. The person who is 'born again' from the Holy Spirit of God is born to eternal life. So this new birth is unrepeatable and has nothing to do with a 'rebirth' into this mortal life. Jesus was not raised into this mortal life either, as was Lazarus (whose skull we can marvel over in France); he was raised into eternal life. 'The death he died he died to sin, once and for all, but the life he lives he lives to God' (Rom. 6.10). So the new life which comes into existence with birth out of the Spirit of God is not in fact a 're'-birth at all. It is the once-for-all and final new birth of a human life for the new, eternal creation of heaven and earth, and the beginning of the fulfilled promise of God: 'Behold, I am making all things new' (Rev. 21.5).

2. Biblical ways of describing the new birth

The classic passage Titus 3.5–7 explains rebirth (or 'regeneration') as 'renewal', using this as a way of describing the baptismal experience of faith, or faith's experience of baptism through Spirit and water: 'He saved us . . . in virtue of his own mercy, by the washing of regeneration [rebirth] and renewal in the Holy Spirit, which he poured out upon us richly through Jesus Christ our Saviour, so that through him we might be justified by his grace and become heirs in hope of eternal life.' The theological formula used in I Peter 1.3–4 for the experience of baptism is very similar: 'Blessed be the God and Father of our Lord Jesus Christ, by whom we have been born anew to a living hope through the resurrection of Jesus Christ from the dead, to an inheritance which is imperishable, undefiled, and unfading, kept in heaven for you . . .' What has happened? A person believes in Christ and recognizes in Jesus the Saviour. He or she is baptized in Christ's congregation. Their personal experience belongs from the very outset within the social experience of the Christian community. Baptism is a happening to the individual and for the individual – but in the congregation.

The new birth takes place 'through the Holy Spirit' or 'through the resurrection of Jesus Christ from the dead'; for the renewing Holy Spirit is 'the power of the resurrection from the dead' (cf. Rom. 8.11). Its motivating power is God's 'mercy'. The Hebrew word used here shows that this means love as strong as labour pains. God's compassion is creative and gives birth to new life.

The historical foundation for this is Christ, or – to be more exact – Christ's resurrection from the dead. It is from Christ's resurrection that the Spirit proceeds – the Spirit who renews and gives birth to new life, and who lays hold of us in faith. For the forgiveness of sins, we are pointed to Christ's death on the cross and its meaning for salvation; but the saving significance of his resurrection from the dead is manifested and expressed in our 'rebirth to a living hope'. New life begins in us through the power of hope: that is an Easter experience. In this experience believers no longer feel themselves sinners cut off from God. They now find themselves people who have been 'made righteous' and as children and fellow householders accepted by God. In the forgiveness of sins, 'righteousness' is a retrospective act – something that points backwards, something that makes good a past that was bad and weighs us down. But in rebirth the righteousness is understood as an act pointing forward towards the future of eternal life: it is the right of God's children to inherit the future shared with God in 'eternal life', in 'the eternal kingdom', in the new 'eternal creation'.

The person who is assured of this inheritance in God's future already lives in 'a living hope' here and now. This is a hope that makes us living people, and a hope that can no longer be disappointed or crushed. The experience of the Holy Spirit makes Christ's resurrection present, and moves us into the resurrection world of eternal life. The remembrance of Christ's resurrection wakens a living hope for God's future, and in this consonance of remembered past and hoped-for future we perceive eternity in time. The moment of 'rebirth' is the eternal moment in which eternity touches time and puts an end to its transience. It is the moment of eternal livingness.

If we look at what these biblical passages are saying, it become obvious that with Christ in faith a wholly new life begins. It is not a restored life, and it is not a rejuvenated life either. It is not even a life reborn out of its origin. The resurrection of Christ has no historical prototype. It is something completely new in history. It is the beginning of the new creation of everything. So the 'rebirth to a living hope' which corresponds to Christ's resurrection in our life in history is also the beginning of a completely new life. We really have to look ahead to the future of God in the power of hope if we want to understand the new character of this life. We mustn't look back to some first, dewy morning of creation which is going to be restored, or to some primordial time when human beings were still holy, just and good. The new birth to eternal life is not 'Paradise Regained'. It reaches forward into the resurrection world which 'no eye has seen, nor ear heard . . . but God has revealed it to us through the Spirit' (I Cor. 2.9f.). The difference is the difference between mortal life here and immortal life there. What is truly new in the 'birth to a new life' is the eternal life which comes into being when our finite life is caught up into the divine life that is eternal. It is always possible for this life to be renewed – perhaps even rejuvenated; but these renewals and rejuvenations are still subject to the thrall of this life's mortality. When a song or poem assures us that 'there is always a May to follow December', it sounds comforting. But in actual fact the precise opposite is true, and ultimately transience triumphs over every hoped-for futurity. A truly new life begins only as the beginning of the new world of the resurrection.

3. *The resurrection joy in personal life*

Is this birth of new life accompanied by special feelings from which we can sense it? Feelings of this kind are of course as diverse and multifarious as people themselves. Nor can we make particular inward experiences a prescribed yardstick for true baptism with the Spirit, using them to test the state of other people's faith. All the same, there are some indications, and in the New Testament believers talk about their experiences quite fully and freely.

The first experience that has to be mentioned is the feeling of rapturous *joy*. When the Spirit of the resurrection is experienced, a person breathes freely again, and gets up out of the defeats and anxieties of his or her life. People lift up their heads, possessed by the indescribable joy that we find in the Easter hymns, and especially in the Easter liturgy of the Orthodox Church. The new birth of life born out of violence and guilt, out of the wrongs and hurts of this life, means a tremendous *affirmation of life*. With the resurrection of Christ out of the finality of his death – 'crucified, dead and buried' – into the breadth of eternal life, God throws open to us, too, that 'broad place where there is no more cramping'. We begin to love life with the love of God which we experience in the Spirit. It far outdoes the disappointments and hurts which reduce our love for life and weigh us down. 'Joy, joy, joy, tears of joy', noted Blaise Pascal on 23 November 1654, in the 'Memorial' which was found sewn into his clothes after his death.

Peace is another experience of God's Spirit in our restless souls: peace with God in Christ, and peace because in the Spirit we sense how deeply the love of God has been poured into our hearts (Rom.5.1, 5). Peace means coming to rest. But it doesn't just mean that. It also means arriving at consonance and concord with God and ourselves. People of peace radiate a quiet assurance. We sense the harmony of their souls. We admire their imperturbability in times of danger. Every human life has its own particular aura. Some people radiate a hectic atmosphere, because they have no

peace in themselves. Others disseminate ambition, because
wherever they are they only look for self-endorsement. And
there are people of peace. When we are near them we, too,
find peace and have a sense of well-being, even if they don't
do anything special and don't attract any attention.

Experiences like this are unforgettable. They stay with us,
even in times of sadness and inward barrenness and desolation, sustaining our existence because they are within us.
Believers are not always happy, cheerful and peaceful, any
more than Jesus was. They are saved none of the torments of
soul which people used to call 'assailments'. The Spirit leads
them into the wilderness just as it led Jesus too. By this I
don't just mean the external lonelinesses. I mean the soul's
dark and desert hours. John of the Cross called them 'the
dark night of the soul', times in which prayers do not just
remain unheard but cease altogether, and no sense of God's
nearness consoles us any more, when God-forsakenness
drives a soul into cold despair, and we can only go on clinging to faith in God in companionship with the assailed Christ
between Gethsemane and Golgotha: 'Not my will but yours
be done' and 'My God, why have you forsaken me?' In times
like this experienced faith becomes naked faith. Faith in God
turns into a faith 'nevertheless'. Then it is important to make
it clear to ourselves that it is not experiences that create faith,
but faith that creates experiences. The firm lodestone of faith
is not provided by the inner experiences of the Spirit, good
and important though these are, but by community with
Christ, in the living and dying and rising again with him.

4. *Remaining and growing in faith*

Can the faith which is grounded in a birth to new life *ever be
lost* or not? Is the assurance of faith also an assurance that
we will remain and endure to the end, in spite of all the
obstacles? This question was often discussed in times of
Christian persecution, for torture often forced Christians to
abjure their faith. Who is free of the fear of becoming weak
and falling in such circumstances? The answer given by

Reformed theology is that true faith can never be lost. Because the birth to new life comes from the Holy Spirit, it is held fast in the faithfulness of God, and never forsakes believers. If it is the new birth to eternal life, then this birth itself is eternal and indestructible. As the power of the resurrection, the Holy Spirit is stronger than death and the terrors and fears of death. The certainty of remaining in faith and not falling is not based on the steadfastness of believers' souls. It is grounded on God's faithfulness to those he has called. 'He will sustain you to the end' (I Cor. 1.8, 9).

Luke's Gospel tells how Peter, 'the rock of the church', denied Jesus three times after he had been arrested, and yet did not lose his faith, for the Lord said: 'Simon, Simon, Satan demanded to have you that he might sift you like wheat, but I have prayed for you that your faith may not fail' (22.31f.). Faith is kept safe in Christ's intercession, even if believers become weak and fall, like other people. To know this is a great consolation. Finally, the Holy Spirit as the beginning of eternal life remains eternally with those who are his, whether they know it and feel it or not. The Holy Spirit 'seals' God's children for the day of redemption. These three statements are not descriptions of the steadfastness of believers. They are declarations about God's faithfulness and his reliability. They are not a reason for self-assurance, but they are a reason for trust in God: even if I am lost to myself, I am never lost to the faithful God. Even if I give myself up, God never gives me up.

If true faith is a birth to new life, there has to be *growth in faith*, too. Every life that is born wants to grow and arrive at the form or configuration towards which it is aligned. Or do we never get beyond the first step of 'Lord I believe, help my unbelief'? There are two different ideas about growth in faith. One of them is the notion about the 'stages' of faith, which correspond to a person's age. The other is the idea about the inner growth of life in the Spirit, 'spiritual life'.

A person's faith has to grow and take on form in line with the different stages of that person's life, which it has to match. There is childish trust in God, there is a youthful

searching for bearings and compass-points in faith, there is
the responsible faith of adult men and women, and there is
also the wisdom of faith in old age. The different experiences
of life influence faith, and faith influences the different
experiences of life. It is dreadful if faith stands still at any
point and is never developed any further. Then quite childish
ideas about faith suddenly crop up in grown-up people.
Often confirmation classes, attended at the age of fourteen,
are the last instruction in faith which people have. It is
exceedingly simple-minded to suppose that this can be
enough for all the experiences of a whole lifetime, until a
person dies. Life in faith must continually address and
come to terms with questions of life and faith. Faith makes
life exciting because we are continually confronted with
questions the answers to which we have to search for.

But growing in faith and the ever deeper, inward
sanctification of life mean something else as well. The future
towards which faith is meant to grow and develop reaches
forward beyond this human life into God's future, 'the day
of Jesus Christ', God's eternal kingdom. The Spirit brackets
together our present with this divine future. That is why we
wait in the Spirit for God's coming, and already experience
here something of God's arrival. That is why at this point
Paul calls the Holy Spirit the pledge or 'down payment' of
that future. The Spirit is the guarantor of what is still to
come. We ourselves sense that God's Spirit is the great
Mover in the direction of the future in which God's glory will
fill the whole world. The Spirit makes our hearts restless until
we come to rest in God's kingdom. According to the biblical
idea, the multifarious gifts of the Spirit are not supernatural
endowments. They are energies of the future, 'powers of the
future world' (Heb. 6.5).

When symbols about 'the birth of a new life' declare that
the people concerned are 'like newly born children', they are
implying that this new life is going to grow and mature. In
this sense there is tested and tried faith, progressions in
the knowledge of God, a strengthening of the will, and an
assurance that is ever more deeply rooted in the heart. Of

course these progressions will always simply be beginnings. Often enough we never get beyond approaches and anticipations. But every beginning reaches forward to its completion. If it didn't, it wouldn't be a beginning. So where do we have to look for the completion of what has begun in us in the new life of the Spirit? Some people have thought of a 'sinless perfection' or perfect holiness already to be achieved in this life. But that is a mistake. The perfecting of our here-and-now new birth in the Spirit will be completed only in the raising of the dead and the life of the world to come. Consequently our knowledge of God here remains fragmentary. It is only when the perfect consummation 'comes' that this fragmentary knowledge will cease (II Cor. 13.10). The completion does not grow out of the beginning, and it does not develop either. It comes to meet us in God's coming. What we experience here in the Spirit as God's *love*, we expect there as God's *glory*. Our growing and waiting in faith, and the eternal life that comes to meet us, are not contradictions, for the expectation provokes the growing: 'Arise, *become* light, for your light *is coming*, and the glory of the Lord is rising upon you' (Isa. 60.1).

5. Is the Holy Spirit our divine Mother?

If the experiences of the Holy Spirit are grasped as being a 'rebirth' or a 'being born anew', this suggests an image for the Holy Spirit which was quite familiar in the early years of Christianity, especially in Syria, but got lost in the patriarchal empire of Rome: *the image of the mother*. If believers are 'born' of the Holy Spirit, then we have to think of the Spirit as the 'mother' of believers, and in this sense as a feminine Spirit. If the Holy Spirit is the Comforter, as the Gospel of John understands the Paraclete to be, then she comforts 'as a mother comforts' (cf. John 14.26 with Isa 66.13). In this case the Spirit is the motherly comforter of her children. Linguistically this brings out the feminine form of Yahweh's *ruach* in Hebrew. Spirit is feminine in Hebrew, neuter in Greek, and masculine in Latin and German.

The famous Fifty Homilies of Makarios (Symeon) come from the sphere of the early Syrian church. For the two reasons we have mentioned, 'Makarios' talked about 'the motherly ministry of the Holy Spirit'. In the seventeenth century, Gottfried Arnold translated these testimonies of Syrian Orthodox spirituality into German, and they were widely read in the early years of Pietism. John Wesley was fascinated by 'Macarius the Egyptian'. In Halle, August Hermann Francke took over 'Makarios'' ideas about the feminine character of the Holy Spirit, and for Count Zinzendorf this perception came as a kind of revelation. In 1741, when the community of the Moravian Brethren was founded in Bethlehem, Pennsylvania, Zinzendorf proclaimed 'the motherly ministry of the Holy Spirit' as a community doctrine for the Brethren. He knew very well what he was doing, for he wrote later: 'It was improper that the motherly ministry of the Holy Spirit should have been disclosed to the sisters not by a sister but by me.'

As a vivid, pictorial way of explaining the divine Tri-unity, Zinzendorf liked to use the image of the family, 'since the Father of our Lord Jesus Christ is our true *Father* and the *Spirit* of Jesus Christ is our true *Mother*, because the Son of the living God is our true *Brother*'. 'The Father must love us, and can do no other; the Mother must guide us through the world and can do no other; the Son, our brother, must love souls as his own soul, as the body of his body, because we are flesh of his flesh and bone of his bone, and he can do no other' (see also my book *The Spirit of Life*, pp.158–9). Zinzendorf then also describes the influence of the Spirit on the soul in romantic terms of great tenderness. And in a German hymn, Johann Jacob Schütz describes the leadings of the Spirit similarly as a guiding 'with motherly hand'.

It is right and good that contemporary feminist theology should have discovered the 'femininity of the Holy Spirit' and reinterpreted it, and it is quite out of place and a sign of ignorance when offical church organs in Germany believe they can scent heresy in this discovery.

Of course the picture of the family of God Father, God

Mother and God Child is no more than an image for the God to whom no image can approximate. But it is much better than the ancient patriarchal picture of God the Father with two hands, the Son and the Spirit. For there God is a solitary, ruling and determining subject, whereas here the Tri-unity is a wonderful community. There the reflection of the triune God is a hierarchical church. Here the reflection of the triune God is a community of women and men without privileges, a community of free and equal people, sisters and brothers. For the building of this new congregational structure, the motherly ministry of the Spirit, and the Tri-unity as a community, are important.

IV

A Meditation on Hope

In front of me I see two angels.

One is *the angel of history*. Paul Klee painted him, and Walter Benjamin interpreted him. His face is turned towards the past. Where we see a chain of events, he sees a single catastrophe, which unremittingly heaps ruin upon ruin. He has turned his back to the future, while in front of him the mass of history's wreckage rises up to high heaven.

The other is *the angel of the future*. The prophet Malachi saw him. He prepared the way for God's coming in our history. This is 'the angel of the covenant', the angel of promise. Mary heard him, and trusted him: 'Let it be to me according to your word.' The aged Simeon saw the fulfilled promise in the messianic Child: 'Now lettest thou thy servant depart in peace, for mine eyes have seen thy saviour.' This angel of the future doesn't look back in grief or anger to our human history with its fields of rubble. He gazes with great eyes into the future of the coming God and heralds the birth of the divine Child. The tempest of the divine Spirit is blowing in his wings and garments, as if that tempest had blown him into our history. He brings the birth of the future from the Spirit of the divine promise.

Many painters have painted this angel of the future, and he has come to meet many of us in one way or another. He seldom encounters us in our successes and victories but generally when our life lies in ruins; for the angel of the future and the angel of history belong together. This angel came to meet me fifty years ago exactly, in a dark, cold hut in a prisoner of war camp near Ostend. As I despaired over the ruin which my people had caused everywhere during the war, I was born anew to a living hope. When I wanted to give up my shattered life, I was raised up by God. When I felt completely abandoned by everything good and hopeful, I found in Christ my brother in necessity.

2

The longer I have lived with this new hope, the clearer it has become to me: our true hope in life doesn't spring from the feelings of our youth, lovely and fair though they are. Nor does it emerge from the objective possibilities of history, unlimited though they may be. Our true hope in life is wakened and sustained and finally fulfilled by the great divine mystery which is above us and in us and round about us, nearer to us than we can be to ourselves. It encounters us as the great promise of our life and this world: nothing will be in vain. It will succeed. In the end all will be well! It meets us too in the call to life: 'I live and you shall live also.' We are called to this hope, and the call often sounds like a command – a command to resist death and the powers of death, and a command to love life and cherish it: every life, the life we share, the whole of life.

Can we learn to hope? I think we can. Because we don't bring this true hope with us from birth, and because our experiences of life may perhaps make us wise but not necessarily hopeful, we have to *go out* to learn hope. We learn to love when we say yes to life. So we learn to hope when we say yes to the future. That sounds very simple, but in the diverse circumstances of life it is very difficult indeed. We experience the power of hope when we have to fight against our apathy of soul. We sense that it is keeping us alive if, when the outlook is sombre, we say 'nevertheless', and dare life. Even if the future of humanity and the earth looks dark, to hope means to live and survive, and to work and fight for the life of creation. Long ago the church father Chrysostom already said: 'What plunges us into disaster is not so much our sins as our despair.' Today we are foundering on our indifference.

True hope isn't blind. It is only the mystical hope for the
redemption of the inner world of the soul that keeps its eyes
shut. The messianic hope for the new world looks into the
future with its eyes wide open. But it sees more than what
can be seen on the horizon of history. The Indonesian word
for hope means 'looking through the horizon to what is
beyond'. True hope looks beyond the apocalyptic horizons of
our modern world to the new creation of all things in the
kingdom of God's glory.

What follows from this is a new way of acting in the
world. In the downfall threatening our world, the person
who looks beyond the horizon to God's new world is
possessed by hope in danger, and confronts danger in the
light of hope. We are then acting para-doxically, in the
literal sense (against the appearance of things), and confuting
failure; for we see more in the hope than eyes see when they
look into the future of the world. We then see this world of
ours in God's kingdom, put to rights and redeemed. In the
struggle for peace against nuclear armaments, and in the
struggle for justice against the dictatorships of violence and
apartheid, many people have been able to say: we do what
we have to do whether we succeed or not. We are acting in
accordance with God's future, the future we hope for, even if
that brings us into conflict with our own society. We are acting out of an inner necessity, in the way that roses flower.
The roses don't ask why either, or what for – they simply
bloom. The same is true of life lived out of true hope.

But the ultimate reason for our hope is not to be found at
all in what we want, wish for and wait for; the ultimate
reason is that we are wanted and wished for and waited for.
What is it that awaits us? Does anything await us at all, or
are we alone? Whenever we base our hope on trust in the
divine mystery, we feel deep down in our hearts: there is
someone who is waiting for you, who is hoping for you, who
believes in you. We are waited for as the prodigal son in the
parable is waited for by his father. We are accepted and
received, as a mother takes her children into her arms and
comforts them. God is our last hope because we are God's

first love. We are God's dream for his world and his image on the earth he loves. God is waiting for his human beings to become truly human. That is why in us, too, there is a longing to be true human beings. God is waiting for human human beings; that is why he suffers from all the inhumanities which we commit personally and politically. God is waiting for his image, his echo, his response in us. That is why he is still patient with us and endures the expanse of ruins in our history of violence and suffering. God isn't silent. God isn't dead. God is waiting. To be able to wait is the strongest strength. God is patient with us and puts up with us. God gives us time and gives us future.

God is waiting for the homecoming of those he has created. God doesn't want to come to rest in his kingdom without them. The great miracle of world history seems to me to be that 'it is not all over with us', as a German hymn says. For this we have to thank God's great, patient, seeking and enticing hope for us and for his whole creation. God is restless in his Spirit until he finds rest in us and in his world.

3

Our great hope in God reaches to the clouds and embraces the whole inhabited globe. It is all-embracing and catholic, in the literal sense; it crosses frontiers and is all-comprehensive. Nowadays this universality is in danger. Today the importance and influence of all the world organizations and their universal values is declining, while the power of particularist group interests is on the increase. Instead of general human rights, people are clinging to the rights of their own community. The rights of one's own country are becoming more important than civil rights for everyone. In the Balkans, the national state is hoisting its flag again, and in the hideous ethnic cleansings is showing its true face, with its contempt for human beings. We are living at the cost of coming generations and are breaking the universal generation contract which has hitherto secured the survival of humanity. Instead of seeking a common life with all other fellow creatures on this wonderful earth, we are exploiting the earth and destroying its living world. Although we all know perfectly well that we can survive only together and in co-operation, today particularist group interests are again getting the upper hand. Some people use the term 'post-modern' when they abandon their concern for the common future of humanity and withdraw into their own histories, calling everything arbitrary or 'multi-optional'. This decline of community is the coming anarchy and is the surest road to disaster.

Not just for our own sakes, no: for God's sake we must not surrender the universality of hope. The church is not there for its own sake, but for the sake of God's kingdom. The church represents God's coming kingdom in this broken and disrupted world if it intervenes on behalf of human rights wherever they are infringed: 'All human beings are created free and equal.' The church represents God's coming kingdom if it intervenes on behalf of this earth as a living world, and gives practical realization to the community of creation. The church represents God's coming kingdom if it stands up for the rights of coming generations today, and makes itself the voice of people who don't yet have a voice of their own. Even if no one likes to think universally any more, the *ecclesia universalis* – the universal church – is called to life through God's universal hope, and represents that hope. The angel of the future is its promise and its defence.

V

The Sanctification of Life

1. What is holy?

The Holy seems to have disappeared from the modern world. The saints have become petrified into statues in mediaeval churches. The modern world is supposed to be a secular world, which has left the sacral world behind it as something obsolete. People are thought to be especially modern if 'nothing is sacred' to them – not an unfamiliar religion, still less their own. Occasionally a journalist can still make the headlines, or briefly raise his TV ratings, with commentaries or stories which would once have fallen under the definition of 'blasphemy' as a statutory offence. But in actual fact no one really gets excited about this any more, because nowadays hardly anyone knows what the 'religious feelings' are which we are not supposed to offend. And yet, the yearning for what is holy and worthy of reverence is still alive in the subconscious minds of modern men and women, and because these longings are unfulfilled, they are even on the increase. For the secular world has the sacral world as its presupposition. It did not itself create this presupposition, and it cannot restore it. It lives from what it denies, because it is its heir. Secularization or profanation is just about as modern and exciting as a man who saws off the branch he is sitting on.

But what is so holy that it has to be sanctified? From time immemorial, what is divine belongs to the sphere of the holy. By this we mean the sublime which we encounter with reverence – the terrible which makes us shudder and which fills us with fathomless amazement – the tremendous before

which we human beings sink into the dust; and not least, that
which fascinates us, holding us spellbound and never letting
us go again. Everything else in our world seems familiar
because it resembles us. But before the Holy we stand
before something Wholly Other, something alien to us which
alienates us from our world. The holy is the inviolable. When
we list the most important characteristics of the holy in this
way, we see at once that what we are talking about is not just
the sphere of the divine; it is the sphere of the demonic too.
And often the demonic initially appears in the light of the
holy as something divine; and then it becomes deadly.

I remember the exalted and fascinating shiver which ran
down my spine as a boy when at school, on special Nazi
occasions, we sang: 'Holy Fatherland, in peril thy sons
surround thee . . .' Then we were ready to die for Germany
– 'You are naught, your people all' – going on with Hölderlin
to say disgracefully about members of the school who had
already been killed: 'And for you, beloved, not one too many
has fallen.' This patriotic mysticism turned 'Germany' into a
terrible and fascinating sanctuary on whose altars the gas
chambers of Auschwitz smoked, and more than twenty
million people died a violent death. The most terrible
demonism, and that in the twentieth century! People who
remember that, or allow themselves to be reminded, will
subject the modern yearning for a return to the holy to an
especially searching examination if they feel inclined to go
along with it. Let me offer some biblical and Christian
reasons for both assent and criticism.

According to all the biblical traditions, God does not dwell
in the holy; the holy is in God. It is not the holy that is God,
or anything divine. God alone is holy – only God and
nothing else. Holiness is exclusively an attribute of God's.
God is 'the Holy One of Israel' (Isa. 43.3), God is holy and
almighty, holy and zealous, holy and true, holy and just.
'Holy, holy, holy is the Lord of hosts; the whole earth is full
of his glory', sing the angels in the prophet Isaiah's vision of
God (Isa. 6.3; Rev. 4.8). According to this, God's nature
itself is holy, for God is always one with himself.

When the Christian creeds call God's Spirit the Holy Spirit, this says on the one hand *who* God's Spirit is, and on the other *what* the Spirit does. The Holy Spirit isn't just one random spirit among the many good and evil spirits that exist. The Holy Spirit is the Holy God himself. The Spirit is not one of God's attributes either, like understanding or will or eternity. The Spirit is God himself in person, no less than God the Father and God the Son. That is why, according to the Nicene Creed, the Holy Spirit 'together with the Father and the Son is worshipped and glorified'. There is no need for us to go into the doctrine of the Trinity at this point. It is enough to know that the Holy Spirit is called holy because in the Spirit we have to do with God himself.

On the other hand we are told in Luther's Large Catechism that the Spirit is called holy because 'he has sanctified and still sanctifies us'. 'As the Father is called Creator and the Son is called Redeemer, so on account of his work the Holy Spirit must be called Sanctifier, or One who makes holy.'

2. Sanctification through God

This means that the word 'sanctification' first of all designates an act that proceeds from the 'holy' God (the older English word for sanctify, 'hallow', brings out the connection between the two words better). God chooses something for himself and makes it his own possesion, which means that he lets it participate in his nature, so that it *corresponds* to him. In so doing he sanctifies it, and in its relationship to God it itself becomes holy.

The first thing that the Creator sanctified, according to the first creation account, was neither an object nor a personal subject; it was a time: *the sabbath*. Why? Because on this seventh day of creation God rested, sanctifying the day through his rest. We find rest only when we are 'at home', in familiar surroundings, the place where we live. This is the way things are on the sabbath: God lives in time on this seventh day, in the seventh year, and in the seven-times-seventh year. This day of rest participates in the divine rest,

and points everything created – human beings and animals –
to the fact that the creatively active and unresting God
desires to come to rest in the rhythm of time, and ultimately
in his eternal kingdom. We are supposed to keep the holiday
– the sabbath, Sunday – holy because it has been sanctified
by God through his indwelling.

God sanctifies the people of Israel by freeing it from its
enslavement in the country of the Pharaohs, with its many
gods, and by accompanying Israel into the promised land of
liberty. God wants 'to dwell among the Israelites'. As Israel's
travelling companion, and as Israel's companion in suffering,
too, God sanctifies the people of his choice and makes it 'a
light for the nations', since from this people knowledge of
God, freedom, righteousness and justice are to come to *all*
peoples – that is to say, the salvation of shalom. That is why
the Christian vision of hope says (Rev. 21.3): 'Behold, the
dwelling of God is with men. He will dwell with them, and
they shall be his people.' What in history is particular to
Israel will become universal in God's future: all peoples and
the whole of humanity will be freed and sanctified, because
the holy God will dwell with them, letting them share in his
eternity and his livingness, as his fellow householders.

What is true for Israel is true for Christians, too. Through
the influence and the indwelling of the Holy Spirit, this
whole throng drawn from all 'the nations' becomes 'the
communion of saints', which is to bring the light of the
gospel to the peoples of the world. The saints are not holy
morally or personally. They are holy as 'justified sinners' –
sinners who have been made righteous – and as strangers
who have been accepted by God. And it is just because of this
that they become the first, preliminary sign and beginning of
the redemption of this unredeemed world. The Holy Spirit
gives them a restless heart which finds rest only in the eternal
kingdom.

The first thing that God sanctifies is always his living
space, his environment. We might say that sanctification is
divine ecology. That is why the temple where God dwells is
sanctified – we call a church God's house too – as well as the

city where the temple stands, and the land in which the
people lives. But the holy space in temple, city and country
is no more than a symbolic beginning for God's grandiose
indwelling of the universe, through which heaven and earth
and everything living is sanctified: 'Thus says the Lord:
"Heaven is my throne and the earth is my footstool; what is
the house which you would build for me, and what is the
place of my rest?"' (Isa. 66.1; Acts 7.49). Holy places on this
earth are holy only as signposts, pointing to the fact that this
earth itself is holy and must be kept holy. God dwells in
space. But the creatively active God does not find rest any-
where except in the new heaven and the new earth where his
righteousness and justice rules. God sanctifies his whole
community of creation through his indwelling. It is intended
to become God's environment and to participate eternally in
his divine life.

In the response of their lives to the Word and nearness of
God, men and women are not just passive objects of God's
sanctification. They are also, on their side, the *determining
subjects of sanctification*. We 'sanctify' something when we
encounter it with reverence and view it as uninfringeable,
because in it we sense and revere God's nearness. The first
object of our sanctification is God himself as he is present in
his Word and Spirit. That is why the first petition in the
Lord's prayer is 'Hallowed – sanctified – be thy name'. The
name of God means God's person which we can invoke, and
God's closeness, his indwelling among us, and God's glory.

The second object of our sanctification is our own life. We
are the subjects of our own lives, in the total form they take,
when God calls us out of our relationships and makes us
persons before himself. As determining subjects, with the
beginning of the new life we take God seriously and try to
live a life that accords with him; for that is what a sanctified
life is. It finds its meaning in its participation in God and its
correspondence to God in the Spirit. This orientation can
take the quite simple form of the question which Martin
Niemöller encountered in a working man, when he was a
child: 'What would Jesus say about it?'– and in the question

of Niemöller's own life: 'Lord, what do you want me to do?'

The all-important things is to seek *harmony* with God afresh every morning, and to hold on to it a whole life long. It is in this harmony that the truth of a human life is to be found. But people who sanctify their lives in this way come up against the ethics of the society in which they live, for God's will is more important to them than the demands and exactions of the people who have the power. Harmony with God means confronting and confuting a world which runs counter to God and itself. For Christians, sanctification means *the discipleship of Jesus* and an inward coming alive in God's Spirit. The Beatitudes and the requirements of the Sermon on the Mount are orientation points for a life in sanctification. These are not arbitrary stipulations. Life in sanctification has to do with a kind of simultaneity with Christ, and this fellowship with Christ has to do with realizing the image of God from our own human side.

Harmony with God is called *sanctification*. Harmony with ourselves as God's image and his children is called *happiness*. In this sense sanctification leads to true self-realization. People who are in harmony with God and themselves are holy and happy. They seek harmony with other people too, as God's image and children, and harmony with everything living which God has created and in which his Spirit is present. Trust in God, respect for our own lives and the lives of others, as well as reverence for everything living, in which God is present: these are the things which characterize and determine the sanctification of life.

3. The holiness of life

What does sanctification mean in the culture of the modern world? Where do we have to rediscover holiness today, and where must we 'profane' what is wrongly considered holy?

I believe that today sanctification first of all means rediscovering *the holiness of life* and the divine mystery in all created things, and defending it against the arbitrary manipulations of life and the destruction of the earth through personal and institutionalized acts of violence. Because life comes from 'the source of life' – the creative divine Spirit – and is alive in the Spirit, it must be sanctified. Life is sanctified when we encounter everything living with reverence before God. The earth is not unclaimed property, as the modern justification of human acts of subjugation and violence maintains; 'the earth is the Lord's, and all that dwells in it' (Ps. 24.1). Men and women can only treat what belongs to God with reverence and solicitude. If they respect God's right of ownership to the earth, then their own rights consist simply of the right to use it. But use must preserve the integrity of property which isn't one's own. Otherwise it becomes usurpation. Because as creator God is present in all the beings he has created, a radiance falls on them from God's glory, and they reflect God's eternal light. We have to keep the life so transfigured by God holy if we human beings want to live. So we shall integrate ourselves again into the warp and weft of life's entire fabric, from which we broke away so that we might dominate it. We shall acknowledge gratefully that we are dependent on nature, but that nature is not dependent on us; for nature was there before us and will still be there when we have gone.

If life itself is sanctified because it is holy, then the conclusion that has to be drawn is an ethic of *reverence for life*, an ethic which Albert Schweitzer taught long before there was any awareness of the ecological crisis. Reverence links a religious attitude towards life with a moral respect for the wonder of life – other life and our own life, too – that is to say, the life common to us all. In order to do full justice to the ecological dimension, we might do well to extend the double commandment of love to the earth, the partner which has hitherto been only tacitly presupposed: you shall love God your Lord with all your heart, and with all your soul, and with all strength, and your neighbour as yourself – *and this earth as yourself.*

Reverence for life always begins with respect for weaker life, vulnerable life. In the world of human beings this means the poor, the sick and the defenceless. In the world of nature it means the weaker animal and plant species, the life of which is at present condemned to extinction because of human barbarism. Today, to sanctify life means defending God's creation against institutionalized human aggression. Laws for animal welfare, plant protection, conservation of the countryside and other protective statutes are necessary wherever our 'fellow creatures' (which is what the German Animal Welfare Act of 1986 calls animals) are exposed to the power of human beings. Today aggression proceeds from industry and from the 'free market'. So it is the function of *a country's government* to protect its *country* and all its inhabitants.

4. *Healthy living and the happy life*

The sanctification of life also has a personal dimension. In the early days of the industrial revolution, the Methodists saw a sanctified life as a disciplined life, without smoking, drinking or extravagant luxury. Today what is asked of us is a disciplined life without environmental pollution, without a wasteful use of energy, and without luxury in what we eat. The renunciation of smoking, drinking and the pursuit of pleasure used to be ridiculed as kill-joy puritanism. In the meantime it has proved to be simply healthy and salutary. 'Smoking can damage your health', we read on the cigarette packets. And the same may be said about the pollution of the environment, wasted energy and an excessive consumption of meat. These things are detrimental to health. We cannot live healthily in a sick, poisoned or contaminated environment.

Today reverence for life requires us to renounce violence against life. Living without violence belongs to personal life, since we have to take the risk personally. But freedom from violence doesn't mean helplessness. To break down the structures of violence against the life of the poor, and to bring about justice in this silent war of rich against poor, is a political task. Living without violence doesn't just mean conscientious objection, important though that personal witness is. It finds practical expression in peacemaking, through the reconciliation of enemies and the breaking down of enmity. Peace doesn't come about because every potential enemy has been annihilated. It comes because enmities are overcome. Living without violence also means minimizing the technological use of violence against nature as far as possible, turning from hard to soft technology, restricting the use of energy by way of more efficient energy production, and caring solicitously for the natural environment.

Not least, living without violence means letting our own lives grow, ending the regimentation of the intellect contrary to the body, and seeking harmony with the body instead of striving for self-mastery. If modern disciplined human beings and men trained to be efficient performers are to recover their health, the reason which has been split off from the whole into an instrument for mere calculation has to be integrated into the reason that perceives, perceiving reason has to be integrated into the receptive senses, and consciousness into the experiences of the body. The modern struggle of the intellect against the body, with its aim of achieving freedom through self-control and self-command, has led – in men especially – to permanent self-mistrust and has inhibited spontaneity. That is why so many people are on the hunt for this very thing at meditation weekends and bibliodrama conferences. Today we find the sanctification of life in the harmonies and consonances of life, which we discover afresh and into which we integrate ourselves socially, ecologically and somatically. As we have seen, sanctification always has something to do with *health*, and health always has something to do with *being happy*. By this I don't mean the health which we feel when we are in a state of general well-being. I mean health as *the strength to be human*. This kind of health can be seen in bodily health and illness, in living and in dying: we need the strength to be human if we are to accept our natural frailty and affirm, not repress, the mortality of human life.

Objectively, the German word *heiligen* – to make holy, 'to

hallow', to sanctify – always has something to do with
heilen, 'healing'; and many languages show that healing has
to do with being made *whole*. In English, holy and whole are
closely connected, and not just phonetically. So the sanctification of life includes the healing of life that is sick, and the
becoming-whole of a life that has become divided and split.
Life becomes holy if it has become whole and complete. So
sanctifying thinking is 'holistic'. thinking. That means the
kind of thinking which doesn't differentiate and divide, as
analytical thinking does, but which tries to understand
the connections and coherences as a whole. The modern
atomization of reality finds an end once we understand that
the beginning is not a single component; it is relation. The
elementary particles are abstractions produced by our thinking, deduced from reality's complex network of relationships. Practically speaking. we need both kinds of thinking;
but the development of the modern sciences has pushed out
holistic thinking, putting it down dismissively as romantic
poetry. But that is unscientific and wrong. We need holistic
thinking in order to understand what we are analysing. Only
we must develop it methodologically.

5. Under the influence of the Spirit

Let us return to theology. God is holy; what God sanctifies is
holy; what is in harmony with God, and thus with itself, is
holy; holy, finally, are the harmonies and concords of living
things among themselves. How do we experience this? We
experience it when in the Holy Spirit God surrounds us from
all sides, and we trust ourselves to his presence and guidance.
Life in the Holy Spirit is a life which lets the influence of the
Holy Spirit *come*. A biblical image is revealing here: 'Now
the *works* of the flesh are plain: fornication, impurity . . .
idolatry, sorcery, enmity, hatred, murder . . . But the *fruit* of
the Spirit is love, joy, peace, patience, kindness, goodness,
faithfulness, gentleness, self-control' (Gal. 5. 19f. and 22f.).
The list that Paul draws up here is influenced by his own
time. In our own situation we could add other things too.

What is important is the contrast between 'the works of the flesh' there and 'the fruit of the Spirit' here. Works are made, but a fruit grows. We cannot 'make' the fruit of the Spirit, nor can we learn it. We have to wait expectantly for it, and let it grow, as fruits ripen on a tree. What becomes real and visible in our lives as 'the fruit of the Holy Spirit' doesn't come from us. It comes from the Spirit in us and through us.

Everything good in us is the 'fruit' of grace. We can open ourselves for it when we ask for 'the coming of the Spirit'. We lay ourselves open to the influence of the Spirit when we give ourselves up to the energies of the Spirit and clear away the hindrances that stand in their way. The influence of the Holy Spirit is not just exerted by way of the intellect, but through the unconscious too; not merely via the will, but also through our feelings and the drives in our lives as well. Existence is sanctified before we do anything at all, for it is the person who does the works, not the works the person. What Paul calls the fruit of the Spirit is as a rule unknown to those concerned. But other people and other living things are very well aware of the peace and the patience, the joy and the trust which radiates from men and women who are filled with the Spirit. These people themselves no longer have any interest in self-contemplation; they have already let go of themselves in trust in the Spirit.

6. The Holy Spirit is the life that makes us live

The experiences of the life sanctified by God and our own holy spirit of life impels us to ask about the nature of the Holy Spirit.

From time immemorial, God's Spirit has been called not just the Holy Spirit but the Spirit of life, for the Spirit does not just sanctify; through its divine energies it gives life. The nearness of God which we perceive in the Spirit makes us wholly living from within, and wakens all our vitality. We already experience here and now the 'giving life to our mortal bodies', which is the way Paul describes the raising of the dead in Rom. 8.11. We sense an unusual lightness of

existence and a buoyancy of life. When we are near the
living God, everything else becomes 'green' and fertile, as it
does in spring, said Hildegard of Bingen. A new passion for
life and a new joy in living take hold of us and all other
living things.

> The Holy Spirit is life-giving life,
> Universal Mover and the root of all creation,
> refiner of all things from their dross,
> brings forgiveness of guilt and oil for our wounds,
> is radiance of life, most worthy of worship,
> wakening and reawakening both earth and heaven
> (Hildegard of Bingen).

So becoming holy means becoming living, and to sanctify
means to make alive.

In this context 'sins against the Holy Spirit' have to be seen
in crimes against life. We 'quench' the Holy Spirit when we
quench life. When the Spirit of life leaves us, all that is left
are destructions, death and desolations. The Spirit of God
who redeems us is none other than the Spirit who makes us
live, for our whole life is meant to be redeemed from the
powers of sin and of death. Eternal life is not a different life
from this one. It makes this life here different, by taking this
mortal life into the divine life, in which it is transfigured and
made immortal.

VI

Charismatic Powers of Life

Every life that is born wants to grow. When someone is born we talk about his or her birthday. Life begins. The senses awaken. The child opens its eyes and sees the light. It begins to breathe, and feels the air. It cries, and hears the sounds. It lies beside its mother and feels the warmth of her skin. The life that we say has been 'born anew' from God's eternal Spirit wants to grow, too, and to arrive at its new form or Gestalt. It is not just our hearts that are born again. So are senses. We see the world 'with different eyes'. The enlightened powers of our understanding wake to knowledge of God. The liberated will seeks for conformity with God's will. The beating heart experiences God's love, and through that love is warmed into love for life. Through trust in God we discover a new trust in ourselves we had never dreamed of. The experience of God's Spirit is like breathing the air: 'God breathes unceasingly in the soul and the soul breathes unceasingly unto God,' wrote John Wesley. In the Spirit God himself is present and surrounds us from every side. We live and breathe in God's atmosphere. So the Holy Spirit becomes the new life's vibrating and vitalizing field of energy: we are in God and God is in us. Our stirrings towards life are experienced by God and we experience God's living energies (Psalm 139). In the 'broad place' of God's presence the new life can unfurl (Ps. 31.8). In this way God's Spirit is experienced as the power of the new life in us, and as the space of the new life round about us.

Life is always specific, never general. Life is everywhere different, never the same. It is male or female, young or old, Jewish or Gentile, white or black. disabled or not disabled,

and so on. What does God's Spirit have to do with this
variety of life in all its specific forms? Aren't we all equal in
God's sight – sinners and righteous, dying and reborn, the
anything-but-saintly and the saints? Whatever we may say in
general about ourselves and other people in the sight of
eternity, the Spirit of life is present only as the Spirit of this
or that particular life. So the experience of the Holy Spirit is
as specific as the living beings who experience the Spirit, and
as varied as the living beings who experience the Spirit are
varied.

Paul makes this clear from the simple event of *calling*:
'Everyone as the Lord has assigned to him, everyone as the
Lord has called him' (I Cor. 7.17). For Paul, call and endowment belong indissolubly together: when God calls someone,
he also endows that person, and he never endows anyone
except for a particular calling. That means that every
Christian is a charismatic, even if many people never put
their gifts into practice, because they fail to recognize their
calling. The energies which a person brings and receives are
perceived in the service of that person's calling; for God takes
people at the point where he reaches them and just as they
are. He always accepts people quite specifically, as man or
woman, Jew or Gentile, old or young, black or white, disabled or not disabled, and so forth, and puts their lives at the
service of the coming kingdom which renews the world. So if
we ask about the charismata of the Holy Spirit we mustn't
look for the things we don't have. We have to discern who
we are, and what we are, and how we are, at the point where
we feel the touch of God on our lives. What is given to all
believers together and equally is the gift of the Holy Spirit
itself. What belongs to each and every person individually
and uniquely is different, and varies: to each his or her own!
In the one Spirit we experience the diversity of the Spirit's
gifts, and in the multiplicity of the Spirit's gifts we perceive
the one divine Spirit.

How do the many-faceted, multicoloured gifts of the Spirit
fit in with the one Spirit? How does the one grace become the
many gifts of grace? To put it in practical terms: how is unity

in diversity achieved without chaos in 'the fellowship of the Holy Spirit'? And how do we arrive at diversity in unity without one person dominating the rest?

1. The vitality of the charismatic community

The question about the different gifts of the Spirit in a congregation is generally treated under the heading 'ministry and community'. But that is misleading, for in the community of Christ all the members have their 'ministry', for they are all 'spiritually' endowed. It is not just the ordained or consecrated ministers who have to be called 'spiritual' ('spiritual pastors'). The Holy Spirit always descends on the whole congregation, and cannot be claimed by anyone as his or her possession. This has been so ever since the first Pentecostal congregation we hear about in Acts 2, even if things have been different in the church's history, and are still different today.

In I Corinthians 7, Paul talks about the *one* calling and the *many* people who are called. All are called to the peace of God without any distinction, but everyone remains in the particular place in which he or she was called (7.20). People are to live as Christians just as they were when Christ called them. Here Paul is thinking about being a Jew and being a Gentile, being a man and being a woman, being a master and being a servant or slave. But when he is talking about these last social differences he adds: 'If you can gain your freedom, avail yourself of the opportunity.' But if not, a slave should feel himself to be 'a freedman of the Lord' and a freeman should see himself 'as a slave of Christ' (7.21). Whatever people are and bring with them is turned into a charisma through the divine calling, because it is accepted by the Spirit and put at the service of God's kingdom. A Christian Jew should remain a Jew and live according to the Torah. A Christian Gentile brings his Gentile culture into the community. Being a woman is a charisma, which must not be surrendered in favour of male ways of thinking and behaving. In social conflicts, too, being a Christian begins at the point where a person is reached and touched.

Why does Paul see what people bring with them as a charisma of the Holy Spirit, even if it is something natural and the result of historical circumstances? Surely these are just the facts of everyday reality? But the Holy Spirit doesn't bring a new religion. It brings new life. It renews this whole natural and everyday life. If a person is seized by the Spirit of life, the whole of personal life becomes a charismatic experience. Life in this Spirit lays hold of the whole of life as it is lived, making it living from within outwards, and transfiguring it. No sector is excluded. It would be denying Christ and quenching the Spirit were I to subtract natural, social, political and physical life from life in the Spirit, and seek only higher 'spiritual experiences'. The whole of bodily and earthly life becomes a spiritual experience when the Spirit of life lays hold of us and we are 'born anew'. It is not just a few specially chosen and unusual people who are charismatics. All believers are charismatics, for the biblical promise tells us that the Spirit is 'poured out upon all flesh' to make it eternally living. These are the gifts given to believers for the tasks assigned to them in their 'reasonable service' in the everyday world, as Paul describes it in Romans 12. We may call them the everyday charismata of the life lived in God's Spirit.

Once it is clear that through calling all individual potentialities and powers are charismatically quickened by being put at the service of love and God's liberating kingdom, we can then go on to ask about the *special* charismata which the Holy Spirit gives to the people who enter into the discipleship of Jesus. These are especially the gifts which people receive for tasks connected with the building up of the community of Christ's people. The community of Christ is for Paul the place where the Spirit is manifested. If we sum up these gifts, we find the *charismata of the proclamation* carried out by men and women apostles, prophets, evangelists, teachers and exhorters; but there are also individual phenomena, such as inspiration, ecstasy, speaking with tongues, and other ways of expressing faith; for there are verbal and non-verbal forms of expression. There are also the *charismata of the diakonia* – the charitable ministry of women and men deacons, people who nurse the sick, people who give alms, social workers, and so forth; just as there are special individual phenomena such as healing, exorcism, the healing of painful memories, reconciliations between enemies, and other forms of help. Finally there are the *charismata of leadership* by 'the first in faith', as these people were called at the beginning – the presidents, shepherds and bishops, both men and women; and also particular phenomena in the context of peace-making and building up community.

These tasks and functions only emerge in the community of Christ's people, so they have to be seen as special gifts of Christ's Spirit. I would not call them 'supernatural', as distinct from the 'natural' gifts we talked about before; for practically speaking what believers do is to put their natural gifts and powers at the service of the congregation, and its growth. But in the service of the congregation they make out of their gifts something different from what they were in other contexts. Together with the tasks with which God and the congregation entrust them, new powers develop in them, powers which they were unaware of previously. But the transitions are as fluid here as they are in real life: the powers employed in the congregation and the powers employed in family, profession and society cannot be separated. They are not subject to different laws. Being a Christian is indivisible. The yardstick in the congregation and 'in the world' is the same: the discipleship of Jesus, which is to say the Sermon on the Mount.

According to Paul's teaching about the charismata, in the community of Christ's people there is unity only in diversity, not in uniformity. It is only the complex diversity of gifts and energies which makes a living and viable unity possible. If it is simply a case of 'birds of a feather flock together', the people who are no different from each other will become a matter of indifference to one another. They make each other mutually superfluous. For the community of Christ, on the other hand, acceptance of other people in their difference is constitutive. Every limitation by way of an imposed uniformity in ideas, words and works is tedious for the congregation, bores 'outsiders' and is anything but inviting. It is only as a unity in diversity that the Christian community will become an inviting community in a society which is otherwise pretty uniform. Creation is motley and diverse, and the new creation even more so.

Paul was living in the enthusiastic springtime of a young Christianity. The first congregations evidently experienced an 'overflowing abundance' of spiritual gifts. Because of that, Paul stresses the *unity* of the community: 'There are varieties of gifts but there is *one Spirit*' (I Cor. 12.4). Today, in our own situation, we have to stress the very opposite: there is one Spirit but there are *many gifts*. After all, it surely can't be true that with us the body of Christ consists solely of one big mouth and a lot of little ears! *Love* must unite the different gifts, said Paul. *Freedom* must release the different gifts, we have to tell ourselves today.

This brings us to a critical question which we have to put to Paul. Must the charismata be judged solely according to their utility in building up the Christian community? 'To each is given the manifestation of the Spirit for the common good' (I Cor. 12.7). Don't the charismata have an intrinsic value in themselves, quite apart from their usefulness for the community? And don't these charismatic experiences of life have a value of their own for the people concerned, before they are pressed into use for the whole? Both these aspects find expression in the praise of the life that has become charismatically living. With this in mind, and unbiassed towards the dispute about today's charismatic movement, this brings us to two particular charismatic experiences: speaking with tongues and the healing of the sick.

2. Speaking with tongues

It is a historically indisputable phenomenon that the birth of the Christian congregations was accompanied by 'speaking with tongues'. This is already reported in Acts 2. Moreover it can hardly be disputed that Christian revival movements have been accompanied by the same phenomenon, and still are. Finally, there is no doubt at all that today the Pentecostal movement is the Christian church that is growing most rapidly, especially in Third World countries. I have no personal experience of this phenomenon, although I have heard speaking with tongues in charismatic congregations in the United States, Africa and Sweden. So I can only judge as a listener.

It would seem to me that speaking with tongues is an inward possession by the Spirit which is so strong that it can no longer find expression in comprehensible language, and breaks out into sighing, shouting and incomprehensible speech – just as intense pain expresses itself in unrestrained weeping, or overwhelming joy in laughing, 'jumping for joy' and dancing. Our services in the mainline Protestant churches in Germany offer a wealth of ideas in their sermons, and have wonderful chorales. But as far as personal forms of expression go, they are poverty-stricken, and offer no chance whatsoever for spontaneity. They are disciplined assemblies for talking and listening. So it is liberating for us to discover in the charismatic worship of black people in Africa and America a completely different body language from our sitting still with folded hands. I would interpret speaking with tongues as the beginning through which a powerful experience of the Spirit loosens the tongues of people who have been dumb, so that they can express what moves them so much. For the people affected first of all, and then for the whole congregation, this is very important. These are personal expressions of a personal experience of the Spirit which exalts the people who are touched by it. And they are new ways of expressing experiences of the Spirit.

We must always be clear that there is no real experience without the appropriate expression of that experience. What forms of expression, verbal and non-verbal, do we in fact have as ways of uttering emotions and experiences of the

Spirit? Speaking with tongues cannot be 'translated', but it can be interpreted, and this too is a gift and a skill which can be found in charismatic congregations.

The awakening of personally experienced and personally expressed faith seems to me to be *the* charismatic experience today. The fact that our congregations listen to sermons but are hardly capable of personal testimony paralyses Christian life and reduces it to silence in encounters with people of other religions. Many Christians are quite content to belong to a church, to 'go to church' occasionally, and to agree by and large with the church's doctrine, even if they don't know very much about it, and it doesn't mean much to them any more. With us the charismatic experience begins with the new self-confidence which lets us say 'We are the church.' Before the mainline churches, the bishops and the synods quench the unfamiliar spirit of the charismatic movement, they should concede to God's Spirit the liberty to awaken men and women, to bring congregations to life, and to seek for forms of expression which are newer than the traditional liturgies. If our bodies become 'the temple of the Holy Spirit' (II Cor. 6.9), a new body language develops which puts us on the move.

Nevertheless we have to put a critical question about the *neglect* of charismata in the present-day charismatic movement. Where are the charismatics in the everyday life of the world, in politics, in the peace movement, and in the concern for ecology? Why didn't they join us in protesting against Cruise missiles? If the powers of the divine Spirit are not given us so that we can flee from the conflicts of this real world into a world of religious dreams, but if they are given us so that we can testify to the liberating lordship of Christ in the very midst of these conflicts, then the charismatic movement must not turn into a non-political private religion. The criterion for life in the Holy Spirit is and remains the discipleship of Jesus.

3. *The awakening of new energies for living*

Many people can do more than they think they can. Why? We are afraid of attempting so many things simply because we are afraid of opposition and defeat. But people who withdraw into their own shells out of fear of setbacks, or because they are afraid of other people's reaction, never get to know their own potentialities. And if we never get to know our potentialities, we never learn the limitations of our powers either. It is only when we go out of ourselves that we arrive at ourselves. It is only when we try to get beyond our limitations that we discover what they are, and accept them. People who do not want what seems to them impossible never fully exploit their possibilities.

'All things are possible with God,' says the Gospel, and who would deny it? 'All things are possible to him who believes,' says the same Gospel, but who dares to believe it in their own case? People can always only do what other people believe they are capable of. We can do things we would never have dreamed of, if other people believe we can. I think of a woman student who was clever, but so shy that she never dared to open her mouth in the seminar. I made her hold the next seminar herself, and she excelled herself and did it very well, because she came out of her shell. Why shouldn't we think ourselves capable of the things God thinks us capable of? Our new energies for living are awakened by trust: by our trust in ourselves, by the trust of other people, by God's trust in us. In the free space of trust our powers are awakened and new powers grow. 'With my God I can leap over a wall,' says the Bible in a splendid image.

If this trust in ourselves is to be strengthened we must awaken our self-love.

'Love your neighbour as yourself,' says the biblical command enjoining humanity. It doesn't say '. . . instead of yourself'. Love of our neighbour presupposes love of ourselves. We cannot love other people unless we love ourselves, and we cannot love ourselves if we don't want to be ourselves but want to be someone else. We can easily make the

counter-check. Can a man who despises himself love the
people he works with? Can a woman who doesn't like what
she is put up with other people? How can we give trust if we
have no trust in ourselves? But self-hate is the torment of hell
for ourselves and our neighbour, too.

True self-love has nothing whatsoever to do with
selfishness, for selfishness comes from the fear of not getting
one's proper share, and of being disregarded. Selfishness is
not self-love. It is rather the reverse side of self-hate. But self-
seeking and self-hate are two sides of the same thing: the
search for the lost self and the inability to accept oneself as
one is. If in faith we have the simple experience that God
loves us, how can we hate what God loves so much? But God
loves us as we really are, not as we would like to be, or don't
want to be. So to love ourselves means accepting ourselves as
God has accepted us, in spite of all the unacceptable things
which we discover in ourselves. In this way we arrive at trust
in ourselves, without illusions or depression about ourselves,
because of our trust in God. God's belief in us awakens our
powers and gives us new ones we had never dreamed of. The
hindrances are seldom to be found in our self-confidence, but
generally in our fear of life, and almost always in an unconscious fear of death. That is why according to the testimonies
of the first Christians it was the Easter jubilation over
Christ's resurrection from the dead that set free the stream of
the Spirit's gifts and new energies of life in the congregations.
The true Pentecostal movement begins with the festival of the
resurrection.

4. *The charismatic healing of the sick*

Apart from the proclamation of the gospel, the healing of the
sick is Jesus's most important testimony to the dawning kingdom of God. According to Matt. 10.8, it is also a commission given to Jesus's disciples. So it is an essential charge to
the community of Christ's people. The experience of healings
in physical and mental illnesses is part of the charismatic
renewal of life. In the context of faith, these healings are

signs of the rebirth of life, and herald the new creation of all things. For in faith, God's Spirit is experienced as the spirit and the power of Christ's resurrection. Healings of the sick are foretokens of the resurrection world which drives out death.

Miraculous, inexplicable healings were common enough in the ancient world. We find them in the world of today, too. In Jesus's case they belong within the context of his proclamation of the kingdom of God, and talk a language of their own: when God assumes his power over his creation the demons are forced to retreat. When the living God comes and indwells his creation, all those he has created will participate in his eternal vitality and will live eternally. Jesus didn't merely express the kingdom of God in words, so as to awaken faith. He also brought it in the form of healings, so as to restore the sick to health. Jesus's 'miraculous healings' are miracles of the kingdom. They are not really miracles at all, but just what we have to expect in the dawn of God's kingdom. It is only if this hope for the coming kingdom that will transform the world is lost that these healings seem like miracles in an unchanged world of death. But in the framework of hope for God's kingdom, Jesus's healings are reminders of hope, and justify expectations of the life-giving Spirit now, in the present. In every serious illness 'we fight for our lives'. In every surprising healing 'life is given back to us' and we feel 'new born'. In the context of sickness the kingdom of God means healing; in the context of death the kingdom means resurrection and eternal life.

Through what power does Jesus heal? What constitutes the healing power of his Spirit? Matthew 8.17 offers us a profound answer: '. . . and he healed many who were sick. This was to fulfil what was spoken by the prophet Isaiah, "He took our infirmities and bore our diseases".' This tells us that Jesus's healing power is not to be found in his lordship over sickness. His power to heal is the power of his suffering. He heals us by carrying our sicknesses, 'and through his wounds we are healed' (Isa. 53.5). When the charismatic pastor Yonggi Cho in Korea sends the sick to his prayer mountain, he makes them write down this sentence many times every day: 'Through his wounds we are healed.'

But how can people who are wounded find healing in his wounds? What is healing? Healing is the restoration of disrupted community and the communication of life. The 'community' of our cells and organs is restored. The community of soul and body is restored. The social relationships which have been disrupted and which are making the person ill are restored. Jesus heals sick people by restoring their fellowship with God, and by his words and his touch he communicates to them the inward vital power of *his* fellowship with God. He heals people who are sick by 'carrying' their sicknesses in his passion, and by becoming their divine brother in suffering. In the picture of the suffering Servant of God, the sick and the dying can recognize themselves, for he recognizes himself in them. Through his suffering and death, Christ brings God's fellowship into the deepest depths of God-forsakenness. He makes sick and forsaken life his own, in order to give it his eternal life. In the Middle Ages, the most moving pictures of the crucified Christ stood in the hospitals for the plague-stricken. Matthias Grünewald's Christ on the famous Isenheim altar is one of them.

5. The charisma of a handicapped life

Accounts of the charismatic movement often sound like American success stories. But the religion of success makes no religious sense in the pains, the failures and the disabilities of life. The theology of the cross doesn't fit this officially optimistic society or its civil religion. But the apostle Paul discovered 'the power of God', not just in the strong places of his life but in his weaknesses as well: 'My strength is made perfect in weakness' (II Cor. 12.9). That is why he boasts of his weaknesses too, the ill-treatment he had been forced to suffer, the persecutions and fears which he had had to endure. For the apostle these meant participation in Christ's sufferings and were a charisma: 'For even if we are weak in him, we shall live with him by the power of God' (II Cor.

13.4). So he expects that in the community of Christ there will be strong and weak, educated and uneducated, people who are good to look at and the plain. No one is useless and of no value. No one can be dispensed with. So the weak, uneducated and ugly have their own special charisma in the community of Christ's people. Why? *All* will be made like in form to the crucified Christ, because the crucified Christ has assumed not just humanity but also the misery of humanity, in order to heal it.

'What is not assumed will not be healed', says one of the principles of the patristic church. But whatever has been assumed by the Son of God who became human and was crucified is then also whole, good and lovely in God's sight. It is important to recognize this divine radiance in the people we call disabled, so that in the community of Christ's people we can overcome the public conflict between the non-disabled and people with disabilities.

The disabled are not just handicapped by mental or physical difficulties. They are also handicapped socially by the strong and effective who put them down as 'disabled'. The disabled can be robbed of their independence, not just when they are pushed out of public life, but also through the solicitude and protective care they are given in homes. If we want to change this we have to stop staring merely at the disablement and see the person who is disabled. Then we can also perceive that every disablement can become a charisma. God's strength is also made perfect in disablements. Those of us who are not handicapped generally stare most at what another person lacks or has lost. But once we forget our own scale of values, we discover the value and dignity of a disabled person and notice its importance for our life together. Anyone who has experienced a disabled person in their own family – and my elder brother was severely disabled – knows how important they are for a family, and can discover what God is saying and doing through the charisma of that disabled person. If the splendour of God's love falls on a life it begins to shine. There are handicapped people in whose faces we can see this light particularly clearly.

Finally, according to Paul the body of Christ – if it is to *be* the body of Christ – needs not just strong members but weak ones too, not just effective and successful performers, but disabled members as well; and God gives the weak and disabled ones the most 'honour and glory' (I Cor. 12.24). Why? Surely because 'the body of Christ' is the community of the Christ who is risen and *was crucified,* who is exalted and *was humiliated.* The astonishing energies of the Spirit reveal God's marvellous power to rise. The weaknesses and disabilities and the sufferings of the Spirit reveal the even more marvellous suffering power of God. For that reason there is no good charitable ministry by the non-disabled to the disabled unless this first of all recognizes and accepts the charitable ministry of the disabled to the non-disabled. Congregations without disabled members are – to put it bluntly – disabled congregations. In the Christian sense, every congregation is a charismatic congregation, and every charismatic congregation is a diaconal congregation; for charisma always means *diakonia,* service or ministry. The great charitable works of the churches are necessary, but what we need is to bring to life diaconal congregations made up of non-disabled and disabled people; congregations which look after their own disabled members themselves as far as possible.

6. *The Holy Spirit is the source of energy and the divine field of force*

The charismatic experiences we have described bring us face to face with the question about the Holy Spirit. Who is the Holy Spirit? And what does the Spirit do?

In charismatic experiences God's Spirit is felt as a *vitalizing energy.* In the nearness of God we are happy and life begins to vibrate. Things begin to dance when we sense that God surrounds us from every side. We experience ourselves and our relationships to other people in the vibrancies of the divine field of force which penetrates us through and through. That is why Greek calls a charisma *dynamis* or *energeia.* From earliest times, the activity of the Holy Spirit of God has been described as a flowing, an outpouring and a shining, that is to say as the elemental quality of water and light. 'Light from uncreated light' floods over us; the Spirit comes like water on to a parched land, so that life can grow and become green. In charismatic experiences God's Spirit is experienced *elementally*, not personally. And from these experiences we can deduce and discern that the Holy Spirit is the source of life, the origin of the torrent of energy.

In the experiences of the Spirit, God is felt as primal and all-embracing presence. God is no longer an aloof counterpart in heaven. In the experiences of the Spirit we perceive a much more intimate relationship than the relation of Creator to creature, more intimate even than the relation between father or mother and child. It is the intimate fellowship of mutual indwelling: God is in us in a divine way, and we are in him in a human way (I John 4.16). In the fellowship of the Holy Spirit the eternal God comes to share in our mortal, sick and disabled life, and we have a share in the eternal life of God. This mutual fellowship is for us an inexhaustible well-spring of strength.

VII

Life's New Spirituality

1. *Spirituality or vitality?*

Today the word 'spirituality' has increasingly come into
vogue. People used to talk about 'religiousness' or even
'piety'. But 'spirituality' sounds more elevated. When we
hear the word we think of retreats and the contemplative life
behind monastery walls. The inward religious experiences of
nuns and monks who renounce the burdens and pleasures of
life in the world and devote themselves to 'the spiritual state'
count as 'spiritual'. They live as celibates and without
possessions, so as to pursue 'the way of perfection' according
to the 'evangelical counsels', unburdened and undisturbed.
Their inner experiences of God are bound up with asceticism
and the rules of the monastic life, with the lesser and greater
fasts, and with regular times for contemplation and prayer.
Earlier, mortifications and flagellation were used, too, for the
sake of the soul's salvation.

If these groups and this lifestyle determine what we call
spirituality today, then a sharp line obviously divides
spirituality from the everyday life of most other people. The
clergy are one thing, the laity another; the Christianity of the
religious orders is contrasted with Christianity in the world,
and religious virtues are contrasted with the civil virtues of
society. So people often set spiritual experiences over against
lower, sensory ones. Whatever is 'spiritual' and 'not of the
flesh' is higher than the fleshly pleasures of the senses. The
one is inward, the other external; the one profound, the other
superficial; the one reflective, the other thoughtless. But the
result is that 'spirituality' sets up an antithesis that splits life
into two and quenches its vitality. In novels and films, priests

and pastors are generally depicted as somewhat unworldly
and cut off from ordinary life, even though through the hear-
ing of confessions and pastoral care they know more about
the shadows and torments of normal life than do the writers
and film-makers.

But is this interpretation of spirituality biblical? We find
nothing of this kind in the Hebrew Bible or in Judaism. There
God's Spirit, Yahweh's *ruach*, is the life-force of created
beings and the living space in which they can grow and
develop. God's blessing enhances vitality and does not
quench the joy of living. The nearness of God makes this
mortal life worth loving, not something to be despised. We
do not find anything comparable in the New Testament or in
Christianity's original messianic traditions either. There
God's Spirit is the Spirit of Christ, and the life-force of the
resurrection of the dead which, starting from Easter, is
'poured out on all flesh' so that it may live eternally. This
doesn't just mean people's souls. It means their bodies too. It
doesn't mean just the 'flesh' of human beings: it means the
'flesh' of everything living. In the tempest of the divine Spirit
of life, the final springtime of the whole creation begins,
according to the Christian hope, and the people who already
experience the Spirit's power here and now sense how vital
and how worth loving their life again becomes. When this
Spirit is 'poured out upon all flesh', the sick, frail and mortal
body becomes 'the temple of the Holy Spirit'.

'The body belongs to the Lord', declared Paul, and who
would contradict him? But he goes on: 'and the Lord belongs
to the body', so 'glorify God in your body' (I Cor. 6.13).
That is unheard of, and has hardly been understood right
down to the present day. It wasn't Paul who talked about
'God and the soul'; it was Augustine. And he did so in order
to leave the body, nature and 'this world' behind. How did
we come to move away from the vitality of a life lived
wholly and entirely *out of* God to the spirituality of a dis-
embodied inwardness, a not-of-this-world life *in* God? Can
we turn back again and rediscover the origin of the divine
Spirit which makes us free to live?

2. *The conflict between 'the spirit' and 'the flesh'*

Paul uses these two terms, spirit and flesh, to describe the
conflicts which are evoked through Christian existence in this
world; but he means something quite different by them from
what spontaneously occurs to us when we use the words.
'Spirit' has nothing to do with the brain, and 'flesh' has
nothing to do with the muscles of our body. Essentially the
apostle was an apocalyptist, and he thinks about world
history in terms of the two great world aeons. Here we have
the transitory world-time of sin and death; there we shall see
the new world-time of righteousness, justice and eternal life.
When God sent the Messiah Jesus into this world, and raised
him 'from the dead', the time of the new world already
dawned in the midst of the time of this old one. 'The night is
far gone, the day is at hand' (Rom. 13.12): that describes the
Christian sense of time.

The ancient and modern, religious and philosophical
apocalyptists say, with T.W. Adorno: 'There is no true life in
a life that is false.' But those who believe that in Christ the
redeemer is already present, and those who sense in themselves the first signs of the life of God's Spirit, know that in
fact true life *does* already exist in the midst of the life that is
false. The future has already begun. The conflict between the
rising sun and the departing shadows of the night is already
being fought out. There is already a struggle for justice
against injustice, and a protest of life against the forces of
death. This conflict is experienced in every Christian existence as a conflict between a life ensouled by God's Spirit of
life and a life which, faint-hearted and apathetic, bears the
marks of the sickness unto death. Paul calls the first life
'spirit', the second 'flesh'. In each case he means life as a
whole, body, soul and spirit. Life 'according to the flesh' is a
life that has miscarried, life that has strayed into contradiction with itself, life which suffers from the bacilli of death.
Life 'in the Spirit', on the other hand, is true life, which is
completely and wholly living, life in the divine power of
life, life which has found the broad space in the marvellous
nearness of God.

The origin of the life that has missed the mark and mis-carried – that which is traditionally called 'sin' – is not located in the sensuality of the body at all, with its allegedly lower drives and needs. It is to be found in the disorientation of people as a whole, and therefore pre-eminently in their souls and wills, if these have surrendered to the death-drive of evil. We all probably find ourselves again and again in such situations, in which we have to live but actually cannot live, so that we surrender to our misery. The origin of true life, on the other hand, is not the soul with its feelings, nor the mind with its reasoning power, nor the will with its determination. It is a person's life as a whole, which comes to its flowering in the nearness of God which that person experiences, and in the warmth of God's love. This touches the body with its senses as well as the soul with its feelings and understanding and will. We could talk about a rebirth to true life out of the life-drive of the Holy Spirit.

Where does this conflict with the negative come from? It comes from what is positive. To the degree to which we sense the first stirrings of true life, we also become aware of the degree to which life has miscarried. In the dayspring colours of their new creation, the things of the world become mani-fest in their unredeemedness. What we had thought was 'quite natural', because we saw no alternative, becomes evident as profoundly unnatural in the light of redemption. With the first experiences of the life-giving Spirit of God we simultaneously hear the deep 'sighing' of unredeemed creation round about us, and we ourselves begin to long for the redemption of the body from the destiny of death (Rom. 8.22f.). We do not yearn at all for the soul to be redeemed *from* its fragile body. What we long for is the eternal coming-alive *of* the body (Rom. 8.11).

Where the rebirth of the whole of life is as Advently near as Jesus proclaimed it to be, then the chains begin to hurt. We can no longer come to terms with them. We begin to rub ourselves raw on them until they break. 'The crime on the streets is not the worst of it,' said a friend in New York. 'What is far worse is that one gradually gets used to it.' If redemption is close at hand, we stop being accustomed to evil; the habit of mind that accepts it is broken. Then we get up out of our apathy and change things. I have always thought that the worst sins of all are to get accustomed to injustice and misery, to make oneself small so as not to be noticed, and no longer to feel the humiliations. 'Bend down so low till down don't bother you no more,' said the black slaves in the southern states of America. But they didn't follow that advice. They fought for their liberty, even though they were forced to suffer in the struggle, and many of them lost their lives.

We shall not be redeemed *from* this earth, so that we could give it up. We shall be redeemed *with* it. We shall not be redeemed *from* the body. We shall be made eternally alive *with* the body. That is why the original hope of Christians was not turned towards another world in heaven, but looked for the coming of God and his kingdom on this earth. We human beings are earthly creatures, not candidates for angelic status. Nor are we here on a visit to a beautiful star, so as to make our home somewhere else after we die. We remain true to the earth, for on this earth stood Christ's cross. His resurrection from the dead is also a resurrection *with* the dead, and with this blood-soaked earth. In the light of Christ's resurrection we can already trace the contours of the 'new earth' (Rev. 21.1), where 'death will be no more, neither shall there be mourning nor crying nor pain any more' (Rev. 21.4).

3. *The spirituality of the soul*

To the extent to which Christianity cut itself off from its Jewish roots and adapted itself to the ancient world, it became a *religion of redemption*. It gave up its eschatological hope and its apocalyptic alternative to 'this world' of violence and death, and merged into the Gnostic religion of redemption. Beginning with the church father Justin, the Greek philosopher Plato came to be revered as 'a Christian before Christ' – he had allegedly 'stolen' his good idea from

Moses – and was extolled because of his sense of the divine transcendence and his feeling for the values of the ideal, spiritual world.

The yearning for the next world now took the place of the messianic hope. God's Spirit was no longer viewed as 'the source of life'; it was now the Spirit who redeems the soul from the prison of the mortal body. In the same measure as redemption was spiritualized, the realm of 'the flesh' was reduced to the body and its earthly drives and baser needs. The Platonic dualism of body and soul and the Gnostic contempt for the body forced Christianity into the mould of a corresponding religion of redemption. It is true that the theologians of the patristic church fought against this tendency. They inserted the phrase 'the resurrection of *the body*' or 'the flesh' into the Apostles' Creed, and called 'the flesh' 'the key to salvation' (Tertullian's phrase was *caro cardo salutis*). But in popular piety right down to the present day, the conflict between soul and body pushes out the conflict between this transitory world of death and the coming world of eternal life. Christian obituary notices also show that the Christian hope for the future of the coming God is continually supplanted by an eternity mysticism centred on a God in the world beyond. The redemption of the soul is conceived of in images of the butterfly that emerges from its chrysalis, or the angel that returns to its home in heaven:

> And my soul spread wide her wings,
> flew through the silent land
> as if she flew towards home
>   (Joseph von Eichendorff).

The consequence was that a mild, non-sensuous spirituality, hostile towards the body, remote from the world, and completely unpolitical, replaced the original Jewish and Christian vitality which lives from God's creative Spirit. Sins are still equated even today with 'the lusts of the flesh', which are identified with licentiousness, although it is patently obvious that the death-drives of this world are to be found in the covetousness and greed for power of the God-forsaken, self-deifying souls of modern men and women.

It was Augustine whose teaching provided the theological foundations for Western spirituality and its 'revolution of the soul', which is called *mysticism*. His theological ideas circle round the one great mystery, 'God and the soul': 'I desire to know God and the soul and nothing else, no, nothing else at all,' he wrote, his conception being as follows: 'When thou art in the soul thou art in the centre; look down, there is the body; look up, there is God.'

Why does the soul of every individual have particular access to God? Because the *image* of God is hidden in the innermost chamber of the soul. Those who perceive this 'mirror of God' in their souls perceive both God and themselves. That is why it is only self-knowledge, not knowledge of the world or knowledge of the 'Thou' in other people, which leads to knowledge of God. The path to knowledge of God leads the seeker to sink into the self. This 'inwardness' is the inner sanctuary in the innermost being: 'Look back into thyself. Truth dwells in the inner being. For in the inner being Christ dwells, and in the inner being thou wilt be renewed according to God's image.' Later, a mediaeval French mystic, William of Saint-Thierry, said: 'Thus does God speak to the soul: Know thyself, for thou art my image and thus wilt thou know me, whose image thou art, and wilt find me in thyself.'

Self-knowledge through contemplation of one's own innermost being gives certain knowledge, because everything that is mediated to me by my senses can be a hallucination. But if I deceive myself, it is still I who am deceiving myself, for the person who does not exist cannot deceive himself. It follows from this that direct certainty of the self is surer than all the certainties about the outside world mediated through the senses. 'Close the gateways of thy senses, and seek God deep within', wrote the Protestant mystic Gerhard Tersteegen in the seventeenth century, in true Augustinian fashion.

The human soul is a deep, unfathomable mystery to itself.

We are related to ourselves and are yet distanced from ourselves. That is why we seek ourselves in everything without
ever finding ourselves. We are deeper than things. It is
because of the presence of the divine Spirit in us that we are
so far beyond ourselves. It is only in us ourselves that we find
this self-transcendence. Only God's Spirit can be more inti-
mately near to me than I am to myself. That is why
Augustine said of the divine mystery that it was 'closer to me
than I am to myself' (*interior intimo meo*), and he confessed
for himself personally: 'Late have I loved thee, and see, thou
wast within me, but I was outside and sought thee there.
Thou wast beside me but I was far from thee.'

Why does the soul seek for God? In their search for God
our souls are only an echo of the God who is in search of
human beings: 'Our heart is restless until it finds rest in thee.'

According to Augustine's ideas, we find our way to God
by withdrawal into our innermost selves. The Western
mysticism that followed Augustine has described in moving
and impressive terms the soul's inner pilgrimage to God.
There are always seven steps, in Teresa of Avila's 'castle of
the soul', or in Thomas Merton's 'seven-storey mountain' –
steps along which the seeker must press, through deserts and
abysses, temptations and torments of soul, until the hidden
'chamber of the heart' is reached, the solitary 'apex of the
soul' where the mystery of the Godhead is revealed. There
the subject of the soul, entering into itself, finds the mirror of
God's image in which at a single stroke we perceive both
God and ourselves. 'The eye with which we see God and
know ourselves is one and the same,' said Meister Eckhart.
In the mutual knowing of God and the soul, the 'mystical
bridal' then takes place. The soul perceives God as it is perceived by him. The mystics were able to call this the soul's
homecoming to God, and at the same time the birth of God
in the soul. It is the ineffable mystical moment.

Every human being is born with a hunger for God in the
soul. Our whole nature is longing, desire, craving. People are
never sufficient for themselves. They always thrust beyond
themselves. Nothing in the created world can still the hunger

for God in their souls. With their longing for God, people
overtax created things and destroy their finite, fragile and
transitory beauty. But all these other created things on earth
and in heaven point beyond themselves to the infinite
Creator, and lead the endless hunger of the soul to the
infinite, which alone can satisfy it.

Human beings are erotic beings through and through, but
their eros can never fulfil its desires in this world because it
is animated and attracted by the infinite beauty of God, the
highest good, and it is only in God that it can find happiness.
If the soul's hunger loses sight of God, it turns to things
which are not God, and is disappointed. Nothing is more
dangerous in this world than disappointed love and love that
has miscarried. Disappointed love for God which has missed
its mark is the power that destroys, the fury of annihilation.
Ever since Augustine, theology has called this 'original
sin'. The soul that is in search of God divinizes things or
powers which are not God, expects too much happiness
and security of them, and by doing so destroys them. Fear
awakens in the soul, the fear that things and other people
will fail to live up to what we expect of them, and this fear
evokes hate of the things and hate of the self; and this hate
generates aggression and acts of violence.

To have seen this is the strength of Augustine's psycho-
logy. Its weakness is that Augustine elevated the soul to God,
but disparaged the body and the senses, as well as nature and
other life. He forged the mutual bond between the inward
and direct personal experience of the self and the experience
of God; but it was only indirectly that he was able to bring
the sensory experiences of 'the other' and the self, nature and
the body, into association with the experience of God.
According to Augustine, the soul's miscarried love for God
leads immediately to the fleshly lusts of concupiscence, the
craving for the base things 'below'; whereas in fact it leads
first to *tristitia*, to *tristesse*, to paralysing melancholy, which
then certainly snatches at compensatory satisfactions, in an
attempt to arrive at happiness just by one's own efforts.

The mystical traditions which followed Augustine pro-

vided one of the essential foundations of Western individualism, for which the dignity of every individual soul is
higher than the dignity of the body, the rights of individual
persons are more important than the rights of the community, and human dignity itself is higher than the dignity of
other earthly creatures. How do these things change if we
trace back the theological presupposition of this mysticism of
the soul and its spirituality to its biblical roots?

4. *New spirituality: life against death*

Who is God's image? According to the biblical traditions,
God's image is not to be found in every individual soul,
elevated above the body. It is men and women in their whole-
ness, in their natural community with one another, who are
God's image: '. . . male and female he created them' (Gen.
1.27). This is a social concept of what is meant by being
made in the image of God, such as has always been stressed
by later theologians – John Wesley, for instance. To keep the
image of the mirror: this tells us that God is not perceived
through self-knowledge in the depths of the individual soul.
He is known in the whole and entire, mutually related, and
hence also bodily and sensory community of men and
women, parents and children, and in other social relationships. It is not just the individual who is to correspond to
God and reflect his vitality and beauty, it is the whole human
community. It is not only the direct experience of the self (if
there is such a thing) which is the place where we encounter
the living God; it is rather the social experience of the 'Thou'
and the responding 'I'.

Is there such a thing as a mysticism of the soul without a
mysticism of the body? No, every good meditation begins
with eutonic physical exercises. Every healing of the soul
begins with movements of the tense body, so that hurt and
sick souls can become one with the body again. Is there a
spirituality of the individual, closed to the world and
other people? Of course to be alone can be a step on the
road to oneself, if society has robbed us of our freedom and

alienated us; but individual spirituality is never there without
the spirituality of the community, just as the spirit of a community is never determined other than by the spirit of the
members. In 'the fellowship of the Holy Spirit', individuals
do not dominate the community, and the community does
not dominate individuals.

The life-giving Spirit must be experienced holistically, with
body and soul and all our powers, and must be sought for
and experienced in community with other people. That is the
promise implicit in being God's image, which is what justifies
the expectation of 'the resurrection of the body' and 'the new
earth'. 'Through their nature, human beings remain wholly
human in soul and body, but through grace they become
wholly divine in soul and body,' said Maximus Confessor,
the Orthodox church father.

For Orthodox mysticism as Gregory Palamas taught it, the
light that shone on Tabor transfigured not just Christ's soul
but his body and clothing too (Matt. 17.2ff.), as a visible
anticipation of the 'transfigured body' of the risen Christ
(Phil. 3.20), into which 'our lowly bodies' will be transformed. A spirituality along these lines cannot have anything
to do with the suppression of the body and the senses, but
will already seek here and now the 'transfiguration' of the
body through the powers of the resurrection, and find it in
the beauty of the whole configuration of life. This comes
about when we open our bodies and senses as well as our
souls to receive the Holy Spirit, preparing them to be his
earthly temple. In the divine love for life we sense how his
eternal living stream penetrates us through and through.

What do we hope for? It is true that the experience of the
life-giving Spirit of God does rouse us to dissatisfaction
with disturbed and false life which has missed its mark, and
awakens an ardent longing for the true life. But this hope is
not turned towards a world beyond this one, or towards
heaven, in a flight from the world in which we live. Our hope
is addicted to the future, and it looks for the coming of God's
kingdom 'on earth as it is in heaven'. Since the raising of
Christ from the dead, the Spirit of God is also the Spirit of

Christ, and the Spirit of Christ is the Spirit of the resurrection of the dead and of eternal livingness. The Christian hope is foundationally and in essence the hope of resurrection. In this it is universal, and expects what Hildegard of Bingen finely calls the ultimate 'springtime of all creation'. This ultimate springtime of creation is experienced here and now in the Spirit in the charismatic quickening of our own life and the life we share.

If we are seized by the Spirit of the resurrection, we get up out of our sadness and apathy. We begin to flower and become fruitful again, like the plants and trees in the spring of the year. An undreamed-of love for life awakens in us; we drive out the sweet poison of resignation, and our painful remembrances of death are healed. We encounter life again like children, in eager expectancy.

5. A new lifestyle

God's Spirit which makes us live does not merely free the soul from its miscarried love. It also liberates the body from its tensions and poisons. The new spirituality comprehends the whole of life, not just the religious sides that used to be called 'the life of faith' or 'prayer life'. The whole of life as it is lived is seized by God's vital power and is lived 'before God', because it lives 'out of God'. What we call prayer in a one-sided way includes rejoicing and complaint before God, and lays before God the life we live and suffer. Faith isn't something special, cut off from everything else; it is the trust in life which finds utterance in all the ways in which we express life. This being so, we can also see this new spirituality as a new lifestyle, a *façon de vivre*.

This new lifestyle can already be found in the earlier forms of spirituality. If we look closely at the famous meditation 'exercises', we find that many of them have nothing to do with an asceticism hostile to life, or with self-lacerating mortifications. They minister to the health of body and soul. Nowadays the fasts of Orthodox and Catholic tradition are prescribed by doctors. Earlier, not to smoke or drink was considered Puritan asceticism. Today it is simply beneficial for our health. Today, forms of environmental pollution should also be marked 'This can damage your health'. There is a *spirituality of the body* which frees the body from the subjugations and disciplines of the soul and the will. We concentrate all our energies on every piece of work we do, investing them for a particular purpose. Consequently, after this tension we need to relax. That was the ancient Jewish sabbath wisdom: 'Six days you shall labour, and do all your work; but the seventh day is a sabbath to the Lord your God; in it you shall not do any work, you, or your son, or your daughter, your manservant, or your maidservant, or your cattle, or the sojourner who is within your gates' (Ex. 20.9f.).

After six working days, people are to rest, and that means not intervening in nature, either nature outside ourselves or our own nature within. On this day of divine rest, men and women will stop looking at nature from the angle of cost-benefit calculations. They will 'let it be' as God's creation, and will enjoy it.

On this day of the week, the nature which human beings process and utilize should be allowed to breathe and come to itself again. Our mental and purposeful concentration on reason and will is relaxed. On this day the mind or spirit can return again to the body which it had made its instrument. The body becomes the temple in which God's Spirit can live and rest.

According to Israel's exilic traditions, the holy place of God's silent presence is no longer the space of the Holy of Holies in the temple in Jerusalem. It is now found in time, in the time of the holy rhythm of the sabbath days. God lives in time, and interrupts the plans and purposes of human labour through his resting presence.

The blessing of the sabbath rest is meant for everyone: men and women, parents and children, employers and employees, human beings and animals. It is not just for the rich, who can afford the time to go on holiday.

The presupposition for the sabbath was once a command to work: 'Six days you shall labour'. But today this com-

mandment must provide the justification for the right of
everyone to work. In this society of growing unemployment,
who still has the opportunity and the good fortune to work
for six days?

It is in the rhythm of the times and the alternation of work
and rest that we find the pulse of life. That is the spirituality
of the lived life. Whatever the mystics sought in solitary
inwardness as the seventh step in the soul's union with God
can be found simply and naturally on that seventh day.

According to the Jewish idea, on the seventh day Queen
Sabbath enters Israel's families and unites God's Shekinah
with the eternal God himself: the Shekinah being God's
indwelling in his people in its wanderings in the exile of
this world. That is the primal biblical image for the soul's
'mystical bridal' with God.

Gerhard Tersteegen found words along the same lines for
the Christian day of rest and its feastday, in which God is
present:

God is in his temple the Almighty Father,
round his footstool let us gather:
him with adoration serve, the Lord most holy,
who hath mercy on the lowly.
Let us raise hymns of praise
For his great salvation: God is in his temple.

It is on this *day of rest* that Tersteegen sees himself sinking
into the presence of God which fills the world like the air we
breathe, or a fathomless ocean:

I in thee, thou in me,
let me see only thee.

Coming to rest on the sabbath or Sunday needs practice. It
has to be learnt. Peace doesn't come of its own accord, and
is not just a matter of doing nothing and vegetating. It is still
true that most family quarrels take place on Sundays, and
most murders in a family on Sunday evenings.

Not least, the political *spirituality of liberation* belongs to
the spirituality of the lived life, liberation of the people we

have oppressed. If we want to be free ourselves, we must free others; if we want to arrive at peace, we must leave other people in peace. True spirituality cannot be a solitary, selfish experience of the self, for every self exists in the network of social and political relationships. If these are oppressive for other people, then liberating inward experiences of self are linked with liberating actions for others. Many people have arrived at their mystical experiences of the self in protest movements and actions for political liberation: con- templation in the very midst of the struggle for liberation and greater justice. In Israel's prophecy, the liberation of the oppressed was part of true fasting and belonged to the laws about the sabbath:

> This is the fast that I choose:
> loose the bonds that you have wrongly imposed,
> undo the thongs of the yoke,
> let the oppressed go free
> and break every yoke.
> Share your bread with the hungry
> and bring the homeless poor into your house;
> when you see the naked cover him,
> and do not hide yourself from your own flesh.
> Then shall your light break forth like the dawn,
> . . . and the glory of the Lord shall be your guard
> (Isa. 58.6–8).

According to Israel's Torah, the earth is also to remain untilled every seventh year, so that it may enjoy 'a sabbath of solemn rest for the land, a sabbath to the Lord' (Lev. 25 and 26). In this 'year of release' for the exploited earth, which today is polluted by so many fertilizers, I see a *spirituality of the earth*: the earth rests, celebrating its sabbath before God, and during this year is not touched by human hands. It comes to itself again and restores its fertility. The land rests and enjoys its peace. Anyone who has once experienced it, knows how important it is to liberate the earth in the sabbath years from human intervention and to respect its own life. In all the so-called nature religions, the earth is rightly called 'mother earth'. In the biblical story of creation only the earth is called 'the bringer forth' of plants and animals (Gen. 1.11, 24). The earth is 'the mother of us all' (Ecclus. 40.1). This does not mean that it is deified; only that its special rights are recognized. Peoples who disregard 'the sabbath of the earth' exploit the land until it becomes infertile, and then they have to leave it, so that it can celebrate its sabbath (Lev. 26.32–34).

Israel tried to interpret its fate in the Babylonian captivity in just this way: because it despised the sabbath of God's earth, it had to leave the land. Only after seventy years of captivity in Babylon was it permitted to return to God's country, which had meanwhile recovered. This ancient story is a warning to the whole of humanity today. If we deny the earth its sabbath and thus its own spirituality, and exploit it non-stop, it will become desolate and void, and humanity will become extinct, so that the earth can recover from human wickedness.

6. *New sensuousness*

True spirituality is the rebirth of the full and undivided *love of life*. The total Yes to life and the unhindered love of everything living are the first experiences of the Holy Spirit. That is why from earliest times Yahweh's *ruach* has been called the source or well of life (*fons vitae*).

If they want to resist the cynicism that manifests itself in the annihilation of the living in the human world and the world of nature, people must first overcome the growing indifference of their hearts. We feel numbed by the mass deaths in Burundi and Bosnia. We accept the mass extinction of animal and plant species without a quiver. But the spirituality of life breaks through these inner numbnesses, the armour of our indifference and our emotional frigidity towards the suffering of others. We can cry out again and weep again. We can laugh again and dance, once this divine love for life awakens in us and the divine Spirit rouses our vitality. Those who begin to love life again like this – and not

their own life alone – will resist the death drives in themselves and the powers of death round about them, and will
fight for the future of life.

If the love for life awakens in us again, our senses also
waken afresh. Rabanus Maurus's Pentecostal hymn prays:

> Our senses with thy light inflame,
> Our hearts to heavenly love reclaim;
> Our bodies' poor infirmity
> with strength perpetual fortify
>   (verse 4).

We may call this *the sensuousness of the Holy Spirit*. How
should we think of it? In a great grief, after the loss of a
beloved child or after a divorce, we feel that our senses have
been extinguished like a candle. We don't see colours any
more. We don't hear sounds any more. We don't taste anything, and our feelings seem to be dead. We become more or
less indifferent, and although we are alive, we are as if turned
to stone. If in the Spirit of life we again experience the unconditional love of God for life, the divine joy in living stirs in us
anew. Then we suddenly see the brightness of the world. We
hear melodies again, our sense of taste comes back, and we
can feel once more. Our senses are quickened and we again
participate in life. This is the sensuousness of the divine
Spirit, who kindles all our senses.

Finally, in order to unfold, our lives do not just need the
strength to live, undivided love for life and sharpened senses.
All these things happen within us. But we also need a
surrounding space for living. That is also an experience of
the Holy Spirit: our hearts are opened wide because we
experience a wide space round about us: 'He also allured you
out of distress into a broad place where there is no more
cramping', says Job 36.16. 'Thou hast set my feet in a broad
room', acknowledges the Psalmist (31.8). What is this 'broad
room' initially, except the unbelievable nearness of God in
the Spirit, which surrounds us from every side? 'Thou
surroundest me from every side and holdest thy hand over
me,' says Psalm 139.5. If the infinite God surrounds our

finite life from every side, then we stand in 'the broad room', and we live and unfold 'in God' as our life-space. We can live in God. According to Jewish traditions 'the broad room' is therefore a secret name for God: *Makom*.

But men and women also give one another living space when they open themselves for each other in love, and when each lets the other participate in his or her life. Loving also means giving time, and conceding space, and having patience with each other, because each has an interest in, and a concern for, the other. That is why the old love songs say 'I am in thee, thou art in me'. Without free spaces of this kind in social life, individual liberty cannot develop at all. Without shared spaces for living, the energy for living in a person's life cannot find expression. Love gives freedom its free spaces.

7. *What do I love when I love God?*

One evening I read the following passage in Augustine's *Confessions* . Augustine says:

> 'But what do I love when I love you? Not the beauty of any body or the rhythm of time in its movement; not the radiance of light, so dear to our eyes; not the sweet melodies in the world of manifold sounds; not the perfume of flowers, ointments and spices; not manna and not honey; not the limbs so delightful to the body's embrace: it is none of these things that I love when I love my God. And yet when I love my God I do indeed love a light and a sound and a perfume and a food and an embrace – a light and sound and perfume and food and embrace in my inward self. There my soul is flooded with a radiance which no space can contain; there a music sounds which time never bears away; there I smell a perfume which no wind disperses; there I taste a food that no surfeit embitters; there is an embrace which no satiety severs. It is this that I love when I love my God' (X.6, 8).

And that night I answered him:

When I love God I love the beauty of bodies, the rhythm of movements, the shining of eyes, the embraces, the feelings, the scents, the sounds of all this protean creation. When I love you, my God, I want to embrace it all, for I love you with all my senses in the creations of your love. In all the things that encounter me, you are waiting for me.

For a long time I looked for you within myself and crept into the shell of my soul, shielding myself with an armour of inapproachability. But you were outside – outside myself – and enticed me out of the narrowness of my heart into the broad place of love for life. So I came out of myself and found my soul in my senses, and my own self in others.

The experience of God deepens the experiences of life. It does not reduce them. For it awakens the unconditional Yes to life. The more I love God, the more gladly I exist. The more immediately and wholly I exist, the more I sense the living God, the inexhaustible source of life and eternal livingness.

VIII

In the Fellowship of the Holy Spirit

1. Fellowship with God?

'The grace of our Lord Jesus Christ and the love of God and
the fellowship of the Holy Spirit be with you all.' So runs an
ancient Christian benediction (II Cor. 13.13). Why is the
special gift of the Spirit seen to be its *fellowship*, whereas
grace is ascribed to Christ, and love to God the Father? In his
fellowship the Spirit is more than a neutral life-force. The
Spirit is God himself in person. He enters into fellowship
with believers and draws them into fellowship with him. He
is capable of fellowship, and willing for fellowship. That is
something special, for we hear nothing about the lordship of
the Spirit here, as we should expect.

'Fellowship' doesn't take by force and possess. It liberates.
We offer a share in our own life, and share the life of
another person. Fellowship lives in reciprocal participation
and mutual acceptance. Fellowship springs up when people
who are different find something in common, and when
something in common is shared by different people. There
are fellowships of shared objective concerns: interest groups,
working parties and study groups. There are fellowships in a
mutual relationship: fellowships constituted by a shared life.
In most human fellowships objective and personal relationships are linked. There is a fellowship between people who
are alike: 'birds of a feather flock together.' But there are
also fellowships between people who are quite unlike. The
people who are unlike find interest in each other, whereas
people who are *no* different from each other soon become
*in*different to each other.

If we remember these different meanings and connotations of human fellowship, then 'the fellowship of the Holy Spirit with us all' becomes a surprising, in fact a quite astounding, phenomenon. In the Spirit, God himself enters into fellowship with men and women: divine life is communicated to us, and God participates in our human life. God acts on us through his enlivening, quickening closeness, and we act on God through our lives, our joys and our pain. What comes into being in the Spirit of life is nothing less than *fellowship with God*. God is involved in us, responds to us, and we respond to God. That is why the Spirit can bring good fruits in us, and why we can also 'quench', 'grieve' and suppress the Spirit. In the Spirit, God is present like a husband, wife or partner. He accompanies us and shares our suffering. The Holy Spirit doesn't deal with us in a domineering way, but tenderly and considerately – in fact, in the spirit of fellowship. This fellowship or community with God in the Holy Spirit is not merely related to persons; it is also objectively related, for the presence of God in the Spirit here and now is the hopeful anticipation, and the beginning in history, of God's presence in the kingdom of his glory.

If it is true that in the fellowship of the Holy Spirit we experience the nearness of Christ's grace and the presence of God's love, not the influence of a divine power, then deeper dimensions still can be found in this divine fellowship. For the Holy Spirit doesn't merely enter into his own fellowship with us, and doesn't merely take us into fellowship with him. The Spirit himself – herself – exists in fellowship with the Father and the Son 'from eternity to eternity', and 'together with the Father and the Son is worshipped and glorified', as the Nicene Creed says. So in the Spirit's fellowship with us is hidden his eternal fellowship with Christ and the Father of Jesus Christ. The 'fellowship of the Holy Spirit with us' corresponds to his eternal divine fellowship. It does not merely correspond to it; it *is* that very fellowship itself. So in the fellowship of the Spirit we are linked with the triune God, not externally but inwardly. Through the Spirit, we are drawn into the eternal symbiosis or 'life-fellowship' of the

Father, the Son and the Spirit, and our limited human lives participate in the eternal circular movement of the divine life. So in the fellowship of the Holy Spirit with us all, we experience the nearness of the divine life, and also experience our own mortal life as life that is eternal. We are 'in God' and God is 'in us'. People who sense this awaken to eternal livingness in the moment of love. In the fellowship of the Holy Spirit the divine Triunity is so wide open that the whole creation can find room in it. It is an inviting fellowship: 'That they also may be *in us*', prays Jesus in the Gospel of John (17.21).

Some people may perhaps find these pointers to the trinitarian fellowship in God speculative. But they have far-reaching consequences when we come to ask: what kind of unity with one another do believers end up with in 'the fellowship of the Holy Spirit'? Is it a personal unity or a collective one?

We might view the Holy Spirit from outside, and interpret it simply as 'the common spirit' of the Christian community. Every community has a common spirit, a corporate spirit, a team spirit or a popular spirit. Why shouldn't the Christian church have its common spirit? This common spirit is always more than the sum of the individual spirits that constitute it, because it represents the quality of the community in which the individuals participate. If we see the fellowship of the Spirit in this way, then the Spirit animates the common life of believers, but the individual members are not shaped by the Spirit as independent persons – only as members. They are not the church; they merely participate in the church. In this participation they surrender their subjectivity and develop a collective identity instead. I don't myself believe, but I participate in the faith of the church. I am not my own 'head'; Christ is my head, because I am a member of his church. 'It is no longer I who live, but Christ who lives in me.' That was already how the apostle Paul explained his new identity (Gal. 2.20).

But are all believers, so very different from each other as they are, no more than 'modes of appearance' of the one common spirit of the church? Are they merely representatives of their common concern? Does the Holy Spirit animate only the life of the whole but not the individual life of believers equally? And who then decides what has to count in the church as being 'the common spirit'? If the community is set above the person in this way, unity rather than diversity will always be given the preference. The love that binds then has a greater value than the freedom that differentiates.

It is true that in the excessive individualism of the modern world we may do well to strengthen community and to stress the things that bind rather than the things that differentiate. But collectivism was never a remedy for individualism: never more than its reverse. People who are always striving only to find personal fulfilment are glad if they can lose themselves and find safety in some great unity; and the converse is true as well. But the fellowship of the Holy Spirit strengthens neither Protestant individualism in faith nor Catholic ecclesiastical collectivism. The experience of the rich variety of the Spirit's gifts is as primal as the experience of fellowship in the Spirit: 'There are varieties of gifts, but the same Spirit' (I Cor. 12.4). The experience of the liberty which gives to each and everyone his or her own (I Cor. 12.11) is inseparable from the experience of the love which binds people together in the Spirit. The true unity of believers in the fellowship of the Spirit is an image and reflection of the Triunity of God, and God's fellowship in differing personal relations. Neither a collective consciousness which represses the individuality of the persons nor an individual consciousness which neglects what is in common can express this. In the Spirit, personhood and sociality come into being simultaneously, and are complementary. Anyone who sets priorities here, putting the one above or below the other, destroys life and 'grieves' the Spirit.

2. The church in the fellowship of the Spirit

When we talk about the church in 'the fellowship of the Holy Spirit', we are presupposing that the community between people and God which is the work of the Spirit reaches out beyond the church. It takes hold of people in Christ's church, and drives them out into the world of the living; for according to the promises in the Bible, the Holy Spirit is 'poured out upon all flesh'. When the church invokes God's Spirit and claims its fellowship with the Spirit, it is seeing itself as the beginning in history of this event. At the very point where the church confesses its faith in Christ, it experiences itself in the wider cosmic dimensions of the coming of the Holy Spirit for the redemption and transfiguration of the world. The church has no monopoly of the Holy Spirit. Nor is the Spirit under its control. The precise opposite is the case: the Spirit binds the church to itself and has the church under its control. The biblical stories about the Spirit show that the Holy Spirit is not concerned about the church. It is concerned about the church, as it is concerned about Israel, for the sake of the rebirth of life and the new creation of all things. So we shouldn't always stress that 'we don't dispose over the Holy Spirit because the Spirit "blows where it wills"'. We should listen to the gale of the Spirit so as to sense where it is leading, and the direction in which it is driving us.

The church's first relation to the Holy Spirit is the *epiklesis*, the persevering invocation of the Spirit, with the plea for its coming. This goes along with our opening of ourselves to the coming of its energies into our common and our personal life. The church above all, which listens to the word of Christ and confesses Christ, exists wholly and entirely in its receptivity for the influence of the Holy Spirit and the radiance of its light. God's word and his Spirit belong together, like God's breathing and his speaking. So there cannot be any substantial contradiction between the Protestant definition of the church as 'the creature of God's word' and the Orthodox idea of the church as the place of the invocation and coming of the Holy Spirit. The two perspectives must complement each other, for where God's word is, there is God's Spirit: otherwise the word cannot be the word of God. And where the Spirit is, God's word speaks to us: otherwise it is not God's Spirit. We may assume that there is a true reciprocal operation or efficacy here. The Protestant order of things – first the word and then the Spirit – is one-sided and wrong unless we think the converse too: first the Spirit, then the word. According to the answer to Question 54 of the Heidelberg Catechism, Christ rules the community of his people 'by his Spirit and Word', not vice versa. Is the reciprocal operation of word and Spirit, Spirit and word important?

The word of the gospel makes Christ present. It thrusts through the times of history to us because it carries the promise of his presence in the Spirit and his coming in glory. The gospel is the remembered promise of Christ. Through faith it creates a community of trust made up of equal and free people, who in the real presence of Christ wait for his redeeming future and hasten towards it. In this respect the church is called to life by the word of the gospel and is sustained in tribulations. Its heart beats wherever Christ finds an utterance.

The Spirit who fills the church is the Spirit of God and Christ. Why did Christ come into this world? So that he might give life. Why did he die and rise again? So that God's eternal Spirit might be 'poured out upon all flesh'. The Word took bodily form so that we might receive the Holy Spirit. 'God became the bearer of a body so that we human beings might be bearers of the Spirit', said Athanasius. Everything in God's history with men and women and earthly creation draws towards the fellowship of the Holy Spirit. The ultimate meaning of Christmas, Good Friday, Easter and the Ascension is Pentecost. Pentecost is the goal of Christ's history, not just an appendix.

So what do we experience in the Holy Spirit? In the Spirit we perceive Christ, and the redeeming fellowship of Christ takes hold of us. In this respect the Spirit is quite selfless, and points away from itself to God's Son. But in knowing Christ and believing in him we come under the influence of the Holy Spirit and feel its energies as the powers of the future world (Heb. 6.5); for Christ is selfless, too, and points away from himself to the Holy Spirit. In the charismatic enlivening of our own lives we experience the coming springtime of the new creation, and we ourselves become a 'living hope'.

For people who experience themselves in the presence of God's Spirit, two different movements follow, movements which are related but alternate:

1. *The gathering of Christians in the church*;

2. *The sending out of the church to Christianity in the world.*

By the church we understand '*the gathered congregation*', which comes together for worship and in mutual trust; and by Christianity in the world we mean *the church as it is dispersed* in families, vocations, jobs and social groups. The meaning and scope of the church is not exhausted when people become 'churchgoers'. It is also present in Christianity in the world. What takes place in the gathered congregation 'religiously' takes place in Christianity in the world in families, and in social and political relationships. Here the church is not represented by theologians. It is represented by Christians in different jobs. Even if these people are called the laity in the context of the church's worship (though that is wrong in itself), where Christianity in the world is concerned they are the experts in their professions, not the theologians.

The mediaeval and Catholic distinction between clergy and laity deprives Christians in the world of their own charisma, and is wrong. The Protestant distinction between 'spiritual pastors' and congregational members is 'uninspired' and just as wrong. In the fellowship of the Holy Spirit there are only 'spiritual' men and women. The long-standing clericalization of Christianity has deprived people in the church of their maturity and responsibility, and ever since the beginning of the modern world it has led to the emigration of 'Christianity in the world' from the official, mainline churches.

The division into clergy and laity and the ghettoization of Christianity in the church must give way to the two vital movements of Christian life: the gathering of Christians in the congregation and their sending out into their different vocations in society. We experience *gathering* and *sending* like the breathing in and breathing out of the Spirit. Christian life in the everyday world is just as important as the gathering of the congregation for worship. We should be forgetting our own calling in the jobs we do and the gifts we have were we to identify being a Christian with going to church. On the contrary, the gathering of Christians for worship serves to build up Christian existence in the different social relationships of life and to give it bearings. The gathering for worship serves the sending into the world, and it is this sending which leads into the full life of the Spirit. Our sending or mission acquires practical form in the needs and distresses of a society whose mark is injustice and violence, oppression and indifference. Every act of Christian worship begins with a greeting in the name of the triune God, and ends by sending the congregation out into the world: 'Go in the peace of God.'

If Christianity is to become aware of what it is, we must abandon the pastoral church which takes care of people, which is the usual form of the Western church. Instead, we have to call to life a Christian community church. Either we set about this church reform by ourselves, or it will be forced on us by the loss of church members. The factors that kept non-voluntary membership of the church going – tradition or milieu – are ceasing to cut any ice. They have already become ineffective in the older Christian churches. Personal and voluntary commitment is going to come to the fore. We can see a sign of this when we note that while traditional Sunday church attendance is dropping, participation in the Lord's Supper or Eucharist is on the increase. More and more Christians are coming to think it important to take over their own lives, to act on their own responsibility, and to experience life in God's Spirit for themselves. The Catholic 'faithful' are now getting up and saying 'We are the church', so that they can play a part in determining the form the church takes, and no longer simply say Amen to priestly services and ministrations.

With this development into the freely chosen participatory church and a personal life in faith, the overtaxed clergy, both

men and women, will be relieved of some of their load –
without losing authority, as many of them fear. For they,
too, are first of all Christians like other people, and like the
rest they have a right to their own lifestyle and their own
personal convictions before they take on the special charges
and ministries of a congregation. They are members of the
community of Christ *together* with the others, before they
stand *in front of* the congregation and act *for* the congregation. Unless they are there *with* others, they cannot be
there *for* others. Without solidarity there is no repre-
sentation. To have overlooked this was the error of the
earlier programme 'church for others'. The community of
Christ is a community of free and equal people (Gal. 3.28f.),
who in the charismatic diversity of their gifts and vocations
live with one another and for one another, and in the unity
of the Holy Spirit together serve the kingdom of God in the
world.

3. The fellowship of the generations and the sexes

In the fellowship of the Holy Spirit Christianity is:
   1. *A fellowship of the generations,*
   2. *A fellowship of women and men.*
   1. Sometimes people behave as if the church were a collection of single, believing individuals. But that is not the case.
It is always and everywhere an assembly of parents and
children, women and men – that is to say, a fellowship of the
generations and a fellowship of the sexes. The community of
Christ consists of bodily people, not bodiless souls; and life's
natural relationships are part of bodily life. It is one-sided
just to talk about a community of brothers and sisters and to
disregard the community of generations: mothers and
fathers, sons and daughters. In pre-industrial village communities the Christian congregation was made up of
Christian families and households, not individuals. The
houses in which different generations lived together were the
'base communities' of the Christian church. Here grand-
parents and parents had their special gifts and duties in pass-

ing on faith and knowledge to the coming generations, and to people living in the same house. Luther's Small Catechism was written for Christian mothers and fathers in their house communities, and even the Reformed churches' more exacting Heidelberg Catechism was also intended for private use in homes.

In the relations between the generations, the function of the Christian congregation is to build up mutual trust between old and young. But the necessary premise is that we also see our fellowship as a fellowship extending over the different stages and ages of life, and so learn to understand others in what they were and as the people they can be, the possibilities they have lived with and the possibilities that are going to offer themselves in the future.

In modern society interest in past or coming generations is appallingly slight. We are experiencing breaches with tradition on the one hand, and on the other breaches of the generation contract through a ruthless imposition of burdens on future generations. Awareness of the present is losing a sense of the present's origins and its future. That is already becoming plain from the fact that people prefer to meet with people belonging to the same age group. The Christian congregation must swim against the tide here, for it is in a position to do so. Of course it is valuable to have groups for children, youth groups, women's and men's groups, and groups for older people; but when birds of a feather flock together, that is not yet a fellowship in the Spirit of God, which spans time. Fellowship in Christ begins first with the acceptance of other people, and interested participation in life that is different from our own. We always think of this in relation to other people living in the same *space* as ourselves, but it applies first of all to other generations in *time*. Earlier, extended families – four generations of them – lived under a single roof. In our modern nuclear families at most two generations do, and among postmodern singles only one. The modern barbarism of disinterest destroys the community of generations first of all, and the generation contract based on that community.

The congregation represents God's fellowship with human beings in the Holy Spirit, and the fellowship of human beings with each other within this divine fellowship. That is a theological statement which we can make clear to ourselves in practical terms from what R. Strunk calls *the building of trust*. Through his Spirit, God confers inexhaustible trust on human beings, and through this trust we ourselves again become trustworthy, however fickle we may be. His word is the word of promise and awakens faith, so that we trust ourselves to him. In bread and wine, Christ puts himself in our hands and trusts himself to us. Through this great trust which God shows us, we acquire a firm trust in ourselves, and trust in our neighbour. Through trust we became capable of fellowship, and prepared for fellowship.

The Christian congregation is a matter of trust. It is a place where we can put aside our natural mistrust and the protective cloak which we don in the day-to-day competitive struggle and fight for survival. Here we can open ourselves and trust ourselves to other people. Of course this makes the Christian congregation highly vulnerable, and often enough a disappointment. The community of mutual trust mustn't be blind and naively credulous. It must be open-eyed and aware, and yet prepared for trust all the same. Christian faith is not a childish trust in God, but has passed through the devastation and abysses of Christ's cross; and in the same way, we only achieve sustaining trust in other people when we know our own weaknesses and accept the weaknesses of the others.

Wherever people live together in trust, there are conflicts. A community of trust cannot aim to be a conflict-free community. Conflicts are not the problem. The problem is their resolution. A conflict that has been suffered through prevents stagnation, and awakens new interest in the other person. Avoidance of conflict results in indifference. So trust is the art of putting up with differences and making them contribute to life. Trust is always ready with an advance payment. But we must also realize that there are limits. Not every community is good and worth maintaining. If it oppresses and stifles people, separation is better. Not all trust is good – only the trust which addresses and comes to terms with justifiable mistrust, and ends it.

2. Human beings are made to be *the image of God as man and woman*. The community of the sexes in space corresponds to the community of generations in time. This is so by nature, and also in history. But what kind of fellowship do women and men arrive at in fellowship with Christ and in the experience of the life-giving Spirit? This is not just a question about organization. Nor is it a question of ethics. It is a question about the experience of God. The first Christian experience of the Spirit was already interpreted early on as the fulfilment of Joel's prophecy (2.28–30): 'It shall come to pass in the last days, says the Lord, that I will pour out my spirit upon all flesh and your sons and your daughters shall prophesy . . .' (Acts 2.17ff.). In the End-time, the life-giving Spirit comes upon women and men equally. In the Spirit men and women will 'prophesy' – will proclaim the gospel. In the fellowship of the Spirit there are no more male privileges, any more than the old enjoy any privileges compared with the young, or independent people compared with dependents. In the kingdom of the Holy Spirit everyone will experience his or her own endowment, and all will experience the new fellowship of free and equal people together. This means that it is impossible to tell women that they have to keep silent in the congregation (I Cor. 14.34). The 'new community of women and men' which is being sought for in many churches today, as the cultural patriarchy comes to an end, is a question of the experience of the Spirit. As long as only men are allowed to be 'spiritual pastors' in certain churches, these churches are 'quenching' and 'grieving' the Holy Spirit.

In churches with a patriarchal hierarchy, the monarchical episcopate rules, with the following legitimation sequence: one God – one Christ – one bishop – one church. This sequence is conceived in purely male terms, and is interpreted as a fatherhood that gives protection and demands obedience.

In the churches of the Reformation, the christocentric

concept of the church is dominant: just as God is 'the head' of Christ, so Christ is 'the head' of the church, and accordingly the man is destined to be 'the head' of the woman (I Cor. 11). This christocentric dogma also led to the exclusion of women from the ministry or 'spiritual office', although from the very beginning the church baptized men and women alike, and by so doing saw them as endowed with the Spirit (Gal. 3.28f.).

Neither the patriarchal nor the christocentric concept of the church has any expectation that the Spirit will be experienced by men and women together, and both repress the Pentecostal experience of the early church.

If we want to do justice to the fellowship of women and men in the church, we must therefore come to have a new understanding of the church based on the shared experience of the Spirit. There is one Spirit, but there are many spiritual energies (charismata). Every woman in the community of Christ's people is endowed through her calling, and every man through his. This endowment through God's Spirit embraces a person's whole existence. To be a woman is a charisma, to be a man is a charisma. The Spirit is 'poured out upon all flesh'. So it brings body and soul to life, and puts the whole person at the service – and sets them in the hope – of the kingdom of God in the world, and the world in the kingdom of God. The different energies of the Spirit act together in the community of Christ for the rebirth of life in the world.

'Prophecy' is called a special endowment by the Pentecostal Spirit. It is an endowment given to 'sons and daughters'. God will speak out of them and through them. This – to put it in traditional ecclesiastical language – is an unequivocal 'ordination' of men and women to the ministry or 'spiritual office'. Men and women are already endowed with the Spirit through baptism. In the fellowship of the Holy Spirit, men and women are charismatically commissioned and endowed to preach the gospel. The patriarchal and christocentric churches face a 'Pentecostal movement' with feminist theology in the vanguard. The ordination of women is not a matter of adaptation to changed social conditions. It has to do with new life from the beginnings of the Christian church: life out of the fellowship of the Holy Spirit.

IX

There is Enough for Everyone

A Meditation on 'Original Christian Communism'

And when they had prayed, the place in which they were gathered together was shaken; and they were all filled with the Holy Spirit and spoke the word of God with rejoicing. Now the company of those who believed were of one heart and soul, and no one said that any of the things which he possessed was his own, but they had everything in common.

And with great power the apostles gave their testimony to the resurrection of the Lord Jesus, and great grace was upon them all. There was not a needy person among them, for as many as were possessors of lands or houses sold them, and brought the proceeds of what was sold and laid it at the apostles' feet; and distribution was made to each as any had need (Acts 4.31–35).

There is enough for everyone! That is the incredible message of this story. We are not being told some historical tale about 'the golden age' of the first Christians long ago. This is the disclosure of real, possible ways of living for us today. We can have this experience ourselves: the experience of the community of the Holy Spirit.

There is enough for everyone: but ten per cent of the people in this country are living below subsistence level. That is the poverty existing in Germany today. How do these things fit?

There is enough for everyone: but millions of men and

women are unable to find work. Mineral resources are getting scarcer and scarcer. Sources of energy are drying up. Prices are rising. Debts are increasing. Want is spreading in all areas of life. What a contradiction!

How can there be 'enough for everyone' when we know that from the very beginning men and women have lived with want, with empty stomachs and thirsty throats, with anxiety in their hearts and fear at their backs? If people have always had to live like this in the past, and will undoubtedly have to go on living like this in the future? There has never been enough, there is still not enough, and there never will be enough. But are we right? Were the first Christians simply being ridiculous? What is the truth?

The Pentecost story is not a new sociological doctrine. It is talking about an experience of God. It is the experience of the Spirit who descends on men and women, permeates them through and through, soul and body, and brings them to a new community and fellowship with one another. In this experience people feel that they have been filled with new energies which they had never imagined to exist, and find the courage for a new lifestyle.

It is a remarkable thing, but whenever people in the New Testament talk about this experience of God in the Spirit of life who makes us live, they become jubilant and fall into superlatives. They talk about 'the abundance' of the Spirit, 'overflowing grace', and the boundless 'riches of life'. Everybody has enough, more than enough, and there is no want any more, not in any way. This is the unanimous experience of life in the Spirit, in the creative, life-giving divine Spirit.

Is this realistic or just religious? Is it a possibility we can actually experience? Or is it nothing more than a beautiful dream, something we yearn for?

We find three factors in our story for the fullness of life and the overcoming of every want:

1. 'And with great power the apostles gave their testimony to the resurrection of the Lord Jesus, and great grace was upon them all.' That is the first thing, for that is the beginning of everything else. It is the resurrection of the crucified

Christ that opens up the fullness of life, eternally living life. Death's power has been taken away. The menaces of death have already ceased to be effective. Everlasting life and life's indestructible joys are already present.

To be in want means to be shut out from the pleasures of life. To be in want means not to have enough to eat and drink. To be in want means to be sick and lonely. In the ultimate resort, to be in want means to lose life itself. The greatest want of all, the absolute deprivation, is death. All the other wants which we experience and suffer from in life are connected with death. They are all something which death steals from life. Because we know we have to die, we cannot get enough of living. But if Christ is risen, that means the spread of hope for life, for a life no death can kill, a life of which there is always enough, more than enough, not just for those of us who are still alive, but for the dead as well.

2. 'Now the company of those who believed were of one heart and soul.' That is the second factor, and it takes us a step further. A collection of people who are quite unknown to one another becomes a community, and these people are at once 'of one heart and soul'. That is what the experience of the Spirit of fellowship means. The Spirit of fellowship is the God among us. In him the divisions between people are overcome. The oppression of people by other people stops. The humiliation of people by other people comes to an end. The estrangement of people from people is swept away. Masters and servants become brothers. Men and women become friends. Privileges and discriminations disappear, from human society. We become 'of one heart and soul'.

Wherever this happens, what is being experienced is really nothing less than God himself. Which God? The 'go-between God' as Bishop John Taylor called him, the God who is community and fellowship, the Holy Spirit. We step out of our solitariness into life together. Our fears of one another and our aggressions towards one another simply become ludicrous, because there is enough for everyone. God himself is there for everyone. He is living here, among us, and invites us through his Spirit of fellowship to become 'of one heart and soul'.

3. 'No one said that any of the things which he possessed was his own, but they had everything in common.' This is the third factor, and everything else comes down to this. In the Spirit of the resurrection hope and in the experience of the God of community and fellowship, no one needs to cling to his possessions any longer. Anyone who has found the assurance of eternal life no longer needs the ambiguous security that possessions give him. So all his possessions are there to be used by the people who need them. That is why 'they had everything in common', and that is why there was 'not a needy person among them'. They brought what they had to the apostles and gave 'to each as any had need'.

Some smart people are critical about this story. They say: 'Oh well, yes, of course – that was primitive Christian communism. But it didn't work out in the end. Human beings just are wicked by nature. They need property because they're egoists. So let's stick to healthy egoism!' They don't realize how dull and stupid – how literally lacking in spirit – their criticism is.

It is, of course, true that when we look at our world, in united Germany, too, we can see that exactly the opposite principle dominates our lives, our busy activities, our economy and our politics. In all these sectors of life the slogan is 'never enough!' Our economy is based on wants. We assume that there are wants everywhere, wants which can only be met by work and still more work, by stepping up production, and by more and more mass products. And those who have to run an economy know that increasing demands must be met with a scarcity of commodities. They also know that this race between growing demand and never-quite-adequate supply is a race that can never be won.

There is never enough for everybody: that's why we have the struggle for oil, the struggle for raw materials, the struggle for world markets, the struggle for educational opportunities and jobs, the permanent hunt after money and pleasure.

Of course there are natural, basic wants which have to be satisfied if people want to live, and if they are to live in decent and humane conditions. But our economy has left these basic needs far behind. It is not these natural requirements that dominate our lives and provide the driving power for our economy; it is demands that have been stimulated and artificially heightened. These additional desires are in principle limitless. They can be stepped up beyond any possible fulfilment. Why? In our modern society human beings have apparently been turned into voracious monsters. They are tormented by an unquenchable thirst for life. They are possessed by an insatiable hunger for power. The more they have, the more they want, so their appetite is endless and can never be appeased.

Why have people in our modern world become so perverted? Because both consciously and unconsciously they are dominated by the fear of death. Their greed for life is really their fear of death; and their fear of death finds expression in an unbridled hunger for power. 'You only live once!' we are told. 'You might miss out on something!' This hunger for pleasure, for possessions, for power; the thirst for recognition through success and admiration – that is the perversion of modern men and women. That is their god-lessness. The person who loses God makes a god out of himself. And in this way a human being becomes a proud and unhappy mini-god.

'There is never enough for everyone. So reach out now and help yourself!' That is what death tells us – death which swallows us up after we have swallowed up everything else. Our modern economy based on want, our modern ideology of growth and the compulsion to expand are pacts with death. They are deadly games with human anxiety. They are bets placed on the craving for life, and they are sucking people dry.

There is not enough for everybody: this motto shatters every human community and rouses one nation against another, and in the end everybody against everybody else, and everyone against his or her own self. It is a slogan of fear, which makes people lonely and leads them into a world which is in principle hostile. 'Every man for himself!' people say. If you don't push, if you go to the back of the queue, that's your own fault. Everyone is his own best friend. And so we have a world that really is without heart and without soul: the dog-eats-dog society.

Finally, this deadly craving for life and this struggle of each against everyone is the very state of affairs we find ourselves in today, when ten per cent of our own people are living in poverty, 700 million people in the world go hungry, and the debts of the Third World nations are driving them into bankruptcy. There is nothing wonderful about this, and it isn't a natural disaster either. These nations are 'underdeveloped' because they have been 'de-developed' – dragged down by the wealthy nations of the world. They are hungry because they are being starved. They are getting poorer because they are encumbered by debt. They are not suffering because of some deficiency of nature. They are suffering from the injustice of other people, the unequal distribution of commodities, unfair prices, and the inequality of opportunities in life.

One can quite well live in poverty. One can even live with poverty. When poverty is shared it is bearable. It is only injustice that turns want into a torment, and being deprived of one's rights that turns poverty into a hell.

If we want to find true life, and to escape the universal death of the world – if we want to gain the true riches of life, and to escape from poverty and want – then we must turn round and begin at the point where the severest loss of all begins: with God. Godlessness leads to the feeling of godforsakenness. Godforsakenness lets the fear of death and the devouring lust for life well up in us; and then there is 'never enough'. But if God is not far off, if God is near, if God is present among us in the Spirit, then we find a new, indescribable joy in living. We are in safe keeping; we are at home; we are trusted and can trust ourselves and other people. Our profoundest want, the want of God, has been remedied. Our yearning for happiness has been fulfilled.

God is present, present in his Spirit. We have to understand this to mean that God is present in our lives as the *living* God. Our limited, vulnerable and mortal lives are sustained and penetrated through and through by God's life, which is unlimited, glorious and eternal. With all the perceptions of our minds, with all the impulses of our souls, and all the needs and drives of our bodies, we are drawn into – we participate in – the eternal divine life. In our existence we feel God's existence; in our suffering we sense God's pain; in our happiness we meet the assent of God's bliss. God is present in his Spirit: 'In him we live and move and have our being.' People who experience and become aware of this, discover how calm and relaxed they become, because they have stopped being afraid, and are encompassed by a great peace.

When the fear of death leaves us, the destructive craving for life leaves us, too. We can then restrict our desires and our demands to our natural requirements. The dreams of power and happiness and romantic far-off places which are used to create artificial wants no longer entice us. So we use only what we really need, and no longer go along with the lunacy of extravagance and waste. For this we do not even need solemn appeals for saving and moderation; for life itself is glorious, and here joy in existence can be had for nothing.

What should we do? I would suggest that the best thing we can do is to build up communities of a manageable size, and to strengthen our sense of the life we share with one another and for one another. The ideology of 'there is never enough for everyone' makes people lonely. It isolates them and robs them of relationships. The opposite of poverty isn't property. The opposite of both poverty and property is community. For in community we become rich: rich in friends, in neighbours, in colleagues, in comrades, in brothers and sisters. Together, as a community, we can help ourselves in most of our difficulties. For after all, there are enough people and enough ideas, capabilities and energies to be had. They are only lying fallow, or are stunted and suppressed. So let us discover our wealth; let us discover our solidarity; let us build up communities; let us take our lives into our own hands, and at long last out of the hands of the people who want to dominate and exploit us.

All really helpful projects or campaigns have grown up out of spontaneous communities at the grass-roots level, not from above: play groups, community aid, care for the poor and sick, and all the many citizens' action groups. The self-help groups of the sick and grieving feel a closeness to Jesus, but not always to the church. The peace groups, ecology groups and Third World initiatives feel a closeness to the kingdom of God, but not always to the church. Ought not the church to accept them as 'bone of its bone and flesh of its flesh', so that it may itself again find the way to Jesus and God's kingdom? In the great bureaucratic organizations of society, the state and the political parties, the churches and the universities, there is always want. But in the voluntary coming together of men and women at the grass-roots level, life's true wealth is experienced. Once all the nations have attained the liberty to provide for themselves before they pro-duce for the world market, there will be enough for everyone to be satisfied.

There is enough for everybody when – yes, when justice is added to the fullness of life, to the powers of life, and to the means of living. Justice ensures that everyone receives 'as each has any need' – no less, and no more.

But the fullness of the divine life makes us all hungry, insatiably hungry, in a different way. And in a different way the Spirit of life makes us thirsty, unquenchably thirsty: 'Blessed are those who hunger and thirst for righteousness.' This is the sector where our tasks for the future are to be found: in the spread of social justice in our own country, and in the creation of justice between the poor and the rich peoples of the world. The poor are crying out for justice first of all, not for prosperity; and we ourselves are perishing from the injustice we permit, even if we are leading comfortable lives. The hunger for justice is a holy hunger; the thirst for righteousness is a sacred thirst. It is the hunger and thirst of the Holy Spirit itself. May that Spirit fill us through and through.

X

'. . . And Thou Renewest the Face of the Earth'

The Ecology of the Creative Spirit

1. The cry from the depths

The beginning of every experience of divine salvation is a cry from the creaturely depths. There is the cry of the tortured people of Israel in Egypt (Ex. 3.7). There is the death cry of the forsaken Christ on the Roman cross (Mark 15.34). And God hears the cry from the depths of misery: God brings his people out of slavery into the freedom of the promised land; God brings his Christ out of death into the life of the future world. Today, the sighs of created beings who want to live and yet have to die rise up to God from the spoiled and devastated world of this earth: 'The whole creation groans in travail together with us even now' (Rom. 8.22). It is suffering from the power of time, and is dying under the brute force of death, and is crying out for the presence of the eternal God in which it can live and endure.

Today an expectation is welling up from the ruined world of this earth. It is the call for the liberating and life-creating power of God. In this cry, threatened creation already opens itself for the coming of God's Spirit. Sadness and expectancy both lie heavy on the whole unredeemed earth. But in the wintry expectation of the spring, the spring of life already heralds its own coming.

What is the distress that makes created beings cry out for their Creator? It is a double distress. It is distress over the inexorable, progressive destruction of nature by human beings, and it is distress over the destructibility inherent in

nature itself: the destructibility that makes this human
aggression against nature possible. Today nature is increasingly subjected to domination and exploitation by human
civilization. But this is only possible because earthly creatures
are subject to transience, to the power of time and the
violence of death. The liberation of non-human nature from
the tyranny of human beings is one side of things. The
liberation of nature from the tyranny of time and death is the
other side of its cry from the depths for life.

The facts and trends of the present ecological crisis are so
familiar, and can be so generally and painfully felt, that we
need do no more than mention them.

The spread of technological civilization as it now is is
annihilating more and more plant and animal species every
year, and in such a way that they can never be brought back
again. It is poisoning the air and the ground, and transforming fruitful earth into deserts. These devastations of
nature, which follow ever harder on each other's heels, proceed mainly from the industrial countries.

At the same time the human population is growing. After
a thousand-year-long equilibrium, it has quadrupled in the
last sixty years, and by the beginning of the next millenium
is going to reach a figure of ten billion people. Human
requirements of foodstuffs and energy are increasing as
rapidly as resources are diminishing. The growth of the
human population is proceeding mainly from the countries
of the Third World.

Injustice and violence have split humanity apart into the
countries of the West on the one hand, and the Third World
on the other; in the Third World they have led to appalling
human and environmental catastrophes. Humanity is caught
up in a vicious circle, in which exploitation leads to debt, and
debt to the using up of the natural foundations which makes
the life of the people in these countries possible. The spread
of human civilization has already reached the limits of the
cosmic conditions for life on earth, and is beginning to
disturb the equilibrium of these conditions. This is evidenced
by the greenhouse effect, which is going to change – and

change lastingly – the earth's climatic zones in the next hundred years. Life on earth is going to be increasingly hard in future. First the weakest members of the community of creation will die – the plants and animals; then human beings will die, too – children, the poor and the sick first of all.

Because we cannot retrieve the poisons that rise up into the atmosphere, or the poisons that seep into the earth, and because we cannot estimate the damage that they will do, we do not know whether human life on earth still has a future, or now merely a present, which is inescapably going to become a past. Because we cannot control the population explosion – and because many nations evidently have no wish to control it – life for most people in the Third World is going to become ever harder, and ever shorter. This is the real, practical misery of living things on earth, a misery which leads us human beings together with all other living things, and as their representative, to cry out to the God who creates life and loves life. It is a deadly misery, which for a long time has made those weaker creatures on earth, together with us human beings, and as our representatives, cry out to the God of life. There is a community of creation, but today it has turned into a community of suffering shared by victims and perpetrators alike, from which there is no escape.

But human beings would not be able to destroy nature in this way were not non-human nature itself frail and destructible. Human beings could not destroy themselves either, were they not are capable of such destruction and were they not themselves mortal. It is evident that earthly creation is no longer in the intact and unscathed condition of its pristine beginnings, about which the Creator could say, 'Behold, it is all very good.' Instead, it has become susceptible to the powers of annihilation. It is evident that present-day creation is not yet in the condition of perfection in which it can abide eternally. It is evident that earthly creation has become subject to the power of time and the brute force of death. That is why Paul calls it a creation 'in bondage' (Rom. 8.22). What we today empirically call nature is no longer the paradise of creation's beginning, nor is it as yet the new, eternal creation. At present sadness lies over earthly creation. A yearning for life torments it. At present we are living in a winter of creation, and are waiting for the springtime of the new creation. What we expect from this renewal of the whole creation is not just that the ravages which we human beings have inflicted on nature and ourselves will be overcome. What we also expect is a transformation of the present conditions of this earthly creation, a transformation of the destructibility of nature, and of our human ability to destroy. The whole creation must be born again to its eternal life, removed from the power of time and the brute force of death. We human beings must be born anew if we are to forget how to commit evil, and are no longer to know death. It is for just such a 'rebirth of the cosmos' (Matt. 19.28) that everything that lives hungers – including us human beings.

Why do all mortal beings cry out for 'the Holy Spirit', and why do all the victims of violence call on that Spirit? According to Jewish and Christian messianic traditions, it was through God's Wisdom in the power of his Spirit that God created all things. Through his Spirit, the Creator is present in each one of his creatures. Through the force of his Spirit, he forms the community of creation. In his Spirit everything comes alive; without his Spirit everything disintegrates (Psalm 104). His eternal Spirit is the driving force and the vital spark in all things. In everything living the passion for life is dominant – and the fear of death. That is why everything living cries out for God's Spirit, in which alone it can live and does not have to die. What exists and cannot endure longs for the eternal existence of God in which it will have continuance. Whatever feels abandoned and destroyed cries out for the Holy Spirit as children cry for their mother, so as to be kept safe. That is why the Holy Spirit is not just called 'the Lord who liberates', but also 'the Mother who gives life' (*'dominum et vivificantem'*). When we wait together with earthly creation for the coming of the Holy Spirit, we are awaiting both things: liberation from injustice and violence, and liberation from time and death.

2. The life of creation

As Christians understand it, creation is a trinitarian process: God the Father creates through the Son in the power of the Holy Spirit. So all things are created 'by God', are formed 'through God' and exist 'in God'. Basil already put it as follows: 'Behold in the creation of these beings the Father as the preceding cause, the Son as the One who creates, and the Spirit as the Perfecter; so that the ministering spirits have their beginning in the will of the Father, are brought into being through the efficacy of the Son, and are perfected through the aid of the Spirit.' For a long time the tradition of the Western church stressed only the first aspect, so as to distinguish God the Creator from the world as his creation, and in order to emphasize his transcendence. By so doing it robbed nature of its divine mystery and delivered it up to desacralization through secularization. The important thing today is to rediscover the Creator's *immanence* in his creation, so as to include the whole of creation in our reverence for the Creator. What helps most here is the christological concept of creation through God's Word, and the pneumatological understanding of creation out of God's Spirit.

According to Prov. 8.22–31 God created the world through his daughter, Wisdom:

> The Lord possessed me in the beginning of his ways;
> before he created his works I was there.
> I was set up from everlasting, from the beginning, before ever the earth was . . .
> Then I was beside him like a master workman, and I was daily his delight,
> playing before him always,
> rejoicing in his inhabited world and delighting in the sons of men.

According to Wisdom literature (Ecclesiasticus, for example), this creative Wisdom can also be called God's Word or God's Spirit. But what is meant is always the presence of God immanent in the world and present in all things. If all things are created by one God, then a transcendent unity precedes their diversity. If they are created by God's Wisdom, then their diversity is also grounded on an immanent unity. Through Wisdom the community of created things is formed, a community in which they exist with one another and for one another.

On the foundation of the experiences of resurrection, Christian theology has seen in Christ both the Wisdom and the divine Word through which the world was created. As the Epistle to the Colossians shows, in Christ it has seen again the cosmic Wisdom through which all things exist. God is the divine mystery of the world. The person who worships Christ, also worships all created things in him, and worships him in everything created.

> I am the light that is over them all.
> I am the All: the All has come forth from me
> and the All has returned to me.
> Cleave a piece of wood: I am there.
> Raise up a stone and you will find me there
> (Gospel of Thomas 77).

Where God's Word is, God's Spirit is, too. According to Genesis 1.2, the vibrant energies of God's Spirit precede creation through the Word. God creates all things through his words, which name, differentiate and judge. That is why everything is individually different, 'each according to its kind'. But God always speaks in the one same breath of his Spirit, which gives life. If we look at the community of creation we see that there Word and Spirit complement each other. The Word specifies and differentiates; the Spirit binds and forms the harmony. When human beings speak, the words differ, but they are communicated in the same breath; and in the same way we can say, in a transferred sense, that God speaks through individual created things and 'breathes through all creation'. Creation as a whole (which I have here called the community of creation) is sustained by the breath of God's Spirit.

Through Word and Spirit, the Creator communicates himself to his creation and enters into it, as the Wisdom of Solomon says (12.1):

Lord, thou art the lover of life,
thy immortal spirit is in all things.

This means that we must not just call creation 'a work of his hands'. It is also God's indirect, mediated presence. Heaven and earth are created so that, as 'the shared house' of all created things, they may become 'the house of God', where God is beside those he has created, and where those he has created can live eternally beside him. For this the Bible uses the image of God's temple:

The Most High does not dwell in houses made with hands; as the prophet says: heaven is my throne, and earth is my footstool. What house will you build for me, says the Lord, or what is the place of my rest? (Acts 7.48f., following Isa. 66.1f.).

The vision of the new creation of all things in Rev. 1.1–6 also adds to the image of the heavenly Jerusalem the idea that in the end the whole world will become the temple into which God's glory can enter and rest. From creation-in-the-beginning onwards, God's Spirit is present everywhere, sustaining, nourishing and quickening all things in heaven and on earth. Its power and its wisdom are at work in everything, giving them duration, life and movement. According to the prophetic and apocalyptic hopes, the new creation of all things will then make heaven and earth God's dwelling place, where he will arrive at his eternal sabbath rest, and where those he has created, as his fellow housholders, will participate in his eternal life and his eternal joy.

If in this way we see God's Spirit in everything, and all things as being prepared to become God's house, the consequence is a cosmic worship of God and a worship of God in all things. What believers do in church is related to the whole cosmos, which they represent. Solomon's temple was already built in accordance with the dimensions of the

cosmos as people then thought them to be: it was supposed
to be a microcosm representing and corresponding to the
macrocosm. The presence of God's Word and Spirit in the
church of Christ is the advance radiance and beginning of the
presence of God's Word and Spirit in the new creation of all
things. From its foundation and by its very nature, the
church is cosmos-orientated. It was a modern and a
dangerous contraction when the church came to be narrowed
down to the human world. But if the church is cosmos-
orientated, then the ecological crisis of earthly creation is the
church's own crisis, for through this destruction of the earth
– 'bone of its bone and flesh of its flesh' – the church is
destroyed. When the weaker creatures die, the whole
community of creation suffers. If the church sees itself as
creation's representative, then this suffering on the part of
the weaker creatures will turn into its own conscious pain,
and it will have to cry out this pain in public protest. It is not
just our human environment that is suffering; it is the
creation which is designed and destined to be 'God's
environment'. Every intervention in creation which can never
be made good again is sacrilege. Its consequence is the self-
excommunication of the perpetrators. The nihilistic destruction of nature is practised atheism.

3. The preservation of creation

Everything created is dependent on the presence of God's
Spirit: 'When thou takest away their breath they die and
return to dust. When thou sendest forth thy breath they are
created and thou renewest the face of the earth' (Ps.
104.29f.). According to Christian understanding, the world
was created out of nothing (*ex nihilo*). So as a consequence
the world is permanently threatened by non-being, and can
only *be there*, and live, through the presence of the divine
Spirit. The Creator must continually secure his creation and
preserve it from annihilation. Tradition expresses this by saying either that God preserves what he has created, or that at
every moment the Creator reiterates his primal Yes to his

creation. The first idea is the notion of the world's preservation (*conservatio mundi*); the second the concept of continuous creation (*creatio continua*). But both ideas are one-sided because both are related solely to creation-in-the-beginning. They do not allow us to think the idea of the new creation of all things. But creation-in-the-beginning and its preservation serve a purpose. And this purpose is the consummation of creation in the kingdom of divine glory.

But it is this divine glory in which everything created longs to have a part. It is for this divine glory that everything created is preserved. It is this divine glory towards which continuous creation points. Creation-in-the-beginning (Gen. 1.1) casts forward in thought to this end, and all suffering creatures wait with longing for this coming (Rom. 8.19ff.). Anyone who wants to talk about God's activity in the world now, in the present, must have this purpose in mind: God preserves those he has created for their perfecting. His preservation of creation in itself already prepares for that perfecting. Every act that preserves creation from annihilation is an act of hope for its future. When we say that 'God's mercies are new every morning' (Lam. 3.23), we are seeing in every sunrise a prelude to the new creation: 'Behold, I am making all things new' (Rev. 21.5).

How does God preserve his creation? God preserves its life-force in spite of human sin and cosmic disorder. God preserves it through his patience, for by suffering all that contradicts life, God gives those he has created time. God's longsuffering leaves those he has created space. The preserver of creation is almighty inasmuch as he 'hopes all things and endures all things' (I Cor. 13.7). This is the way God loves those he has created, enticing them to turn back from death to life, and to return home to his eternal kingdom. If we see the wonder of creation as a communication of God's creative love, then in the wonder of creation's preservation we will see the inexhaustible suffering power of that love. In both these things, God's hope for the future finds expression. Creation's history of suffering is God's history of suffering too. The history of the return to life of created beings is at the same time a history of God's joy over those he has created. For through his immanent Spirit he participates in the fate of what he has created. In the sighs and groans of suffering creation God's Spirit itself sighs and groans and calls for redemption. The God who through his indwelling Spirit suffers with those he has created is the firm hope of created being. This hope is our assurance that the beings he has created have not been forsaken by their Creator.

When Paul talks about 'creation in chains' (Romans 8), and when he stresses the reconciliation of all things through Christ (Colossians 1), the premise is that present reality is no longer creation as it was in the beginning, and that it is not as yet the new creation either. It has become subject to the power of time and the violence of death, and is exposed to annihilation. Whatever reason we may find for this vulnerable condition of creation between its origin and its consummation, the only important thing is the fellowship of suffering which human beings share with other earthly creatures. In our present condition, the community of creation is a community of suffering. Nature will not be saved if it is made part of the human world, and human beings will not be redeemed if they return to nature. In this unredeemed world there is redemption only in the common hope for reconciliation and the new creation of all things.

If we use the term 'nature' for creation's present condition, then nature means a kind of winter of creation. If we follow through this image, the new creation of all things is like the spring, when everything becomes green and fertile, and the ice melts, under which the torrents of life are hidden. Many of our Christian Easter and Christmas carols depict the new creation as the ultimate, eternal springtime of creation.

For the present ecological discussion, this means discovering in our human environment nature in its own independence, and finding in independent nature God's sighing creation. We are accustomed to talk about the 'environment'; but the word is anthropocentric. It means nature only in so far as it is related to human beings. The environment is nature appropriated and controlled by human beings. If we see the whole of nature as nothing more than our own environment, then the underlying intention is nothing other than the total dissolution of nature's independence. The desacralization of nature is followed by its degradation, its reduction to an environment for human beings. In this respect the word environment is a highly aggressive term. It could well be that nature will react in an unpleasant way and will begin its own counter-evolutions. So it is vitally necessary to rediscover behind our own environment nature as an independent subject with its own rights. 'Every form of life is unique, warranting respect regardless of its worth for man,' says the UNO World Charter for Nature of 1982, rightly.

Human culture must be 'environmentally compatible'; but the human environment must also be 'nature-compatible' and must take into account nature's laws and rhythms, as well as the natural environments of other living things: plants, trees and animals. It is only when nature's own rights are respected that we can discover the inner side of nature which we call creation: the side turned towards God. Nature is the present, immanent side of creation. Creation is the transcendent side of nature. That means that inherent in every natural being is an immanent transcendence, and that transcendence is immanent in every natural being. When we call the reality in which and with which we live 'creation', this is the strongest possible way of expressing resistance to the transformation of nature into human environment, and uttering our opposition to its destruction. The resistance springs from hope for creation's liberation from its present natural condition for the eternal springtime of the new world. It is not just resistance against the ecological self-destruction of humanity which is annihilating the foundations of its own life. It is resistance against the fetters of humanity's frailty, and humanity's sadness.

4. *The rebirth of creation from the Spirit of God*

The final new creation of all things goes far beyond the daily preservation of creation. The new creation will overcome not only the destruction but also the destructibility; not just death through human violence, but the mortality of created being itself. The fundamental conditions of present creation will be transformed. Creation will be freed from the power of time for the presence of eternity, and from the power of death for eternal life. The creation which is everywhere threatened by chaos and annihilation will be kept wholly safe and secure in God's eternal love.

Christ proclaimed this new creation of all things when he brought God's kingdom to the poor, and God's salvation to the sick, and God's justice to sinners. For the Christian hope, this new creation of all things begins with the raising of Christ from the dead, and with the overcoming of death's power through his resurrection.

As Christians see it, the day of Christ's resurrection is the first day of the new creation. That is why it begins with the new creation of light: 'The God who said "Let light shine out of darkness" has shone in our hearts to give the light of the knowledge of the glory of God in the face of Jesus Christ' (II Cor. 4.6). According to what the witnesses tell us, the 'Easter appearances' took place in the cosmic light of the first day of the new creation. That is why, early on, Christians called the day of resurrection 'the eighth day' – that is to say the first day of the new creation. They understood Christ's resurrection in cosmic dimensions – not merely in historical ones – as the beginning of the new world in which all tears will be wiped away and death will be no more.

It is in this sense that the Orthodox Easter liturgy proclaims:

Now all is filled with light,
heaven and earth and the realm of the dead.
The whole creation rejoices in Christ's resurrection, which is its true foundation.

The hymn-writers of the Western church speak the same language, for example Venantius Fortunatus.

Earth with joy confesses, clothing her for spring,
All good gifts restored with her returning King.
Bloom in every meadow, leaves on every bough,
speak his sorrows ended, hail his triumph now.

It is not by chance that with us the Christian festival of Easter coincides with the festival of spring. The springtime of nature was interpreted as the symbol of the eternal springtime of the new creation of all things. Nor is it by chance that the Christian feast of Pentecost coincides with the beginning of summer. The greening and flowering of nature was seen as a symbol of the eternal quickening of the whole creation in the breath of the divine Spirit. With the raising of Christ from the dead and the annihilation of death which took place in him, the eschatological process of the new creation of all transient and mortal beings begins. Whoever out of the deadly perils of earthly creation cries out for the Creator Spirit expects with the resurrection of Christ the resurrection of the body and the resurrection of nature also.

With the rebirth of Christ from death to eternal life we also expect the rebirth of the whole cosmos. Nothing that God has created is lost. Everything returns in transfigured form. So we expect that the Spirit of the new creation of all things will vanquish human violence and cosmic chaos. More than that: we expect that the power of time and the power of death will be vanquished, too. Finally, we expect eternal consolation when 'the tears are wiped away' from our eyes. We expect eternal joy in the dance of fellowship with all created being and with the triune God.

We summon up many images in an attempt to imagine this new creation of all things for which we long. These images are all strong in their denial of the negative from which we suffer: 'There shall be no mourning nor crying nor pain any more', for God 'will wipe away every tear from their eyes, and death shall be no more' (Rev. 21.4). But they are feeble in their picture of the positive side, because in this impaired life we can as yet have no experience of the new creation. And yet without anticipations of the positive, we cannot form any notion of the negative. We suffer because we love; we are afraid of dying because we want to live; we want to remain and not to pass away. Out of the positive experiences of love, of life, of permanence, we put together the picture of hope for the new creation of all things. That is why we talk about 'the kingdom of God' which is going to drive out the forces of chaos. That is why we talk about the 'eternal life' which is going to overcome death. That is why we hope for 'the divine righteousness and justice' which is going to drive injustice and violence from the face of the earth. That is why we try to hope for the resurrection of created beings that have died, and for their rebirth to eternal life. Otherwise we should despair over the mass death that is round about us every day.

Out of hope for eternal life, love for this vulnerable and mortal life is born afresh. This love does not give anything up. If we had to surrender hope for as much as one single creature, for us Christ would not have risen. The love founded on hope is the strongest medicine against the spreading sickness of resignation. The modern cynicism which is prepared to accept the death of so many created things is an ally of death. But we Christians are what Christoph Blumhardt called 'protest-people against death'. That is why out of the deadly depths we cry out for God's Spirit. That is why we cry out for the Spirit who sustains the whole creation, and wait for the Spirit of the new creation of all things. Our cry from the depths is a sign of life – a sign of divine life.

XI

What Are We Doing When We Pray?

My God,
we cry out and complain
  we groan and weep
    we are speechless and silent.
And we beg and implore,
  we wish and we will,
    we crave and insist.
We thank and praise,
  we rejoice and dance,
    we sing and we glorify.

These are all ways of expressing our lives before God. To call
them all 'praying' is much too narrow, because the word
'pray' means much the same as 'ask' and 'plead'. But to come
to God only with our entreaties is hardly the expression of a
true love for God. God is more than our heavenly helper in
time of need.

God is our Father because he is the intimate Abba mystery
of Jesus, who became our brother. Only hired servants beg
from their masters. Children talk trustfully and confidently
to their mothers and fathers about the things that are on their
minds. As we do in a family, we tell God about our joys and
our suffering because we know how lovingly God shares in
our lives; for God is a lover of life (Wisdom 11.26). Only
servants come to their masters solely with their requests and
demands, otherwise preferring to keep well away from them.
'Needs must', they say, and when it is a question of their own
distresses they seek out their 'helpers in time of need'; but
they show no concern for the 'helpers' themselves.

Friends don't behave to each other like this. They tell one another their joys, and then their sorrows too. Only the person who can share the rejoicing can also suffer in sympathy when it comes to the point. Friends advise each other in difficulty, when it is a matter of vital importance. They are bonded to each other in affection and respect. Their affection doesn't smother their friend. Their respect for the other person's liberty never turns into indifference. We pour out our hearts to God as we do to an understanding friend. And when we pray for other people, or tell God our wants and desires, we are advising him in his government of the world. But we don't *coerce* our 'heavenly friend' with our plans and intentions; we respect his freedom. Talking to God and listening to him in this freedom, which is the expression of great love, is 'prayer in the Holy Spirit'. This is the way God's friends pray. It is true that in the Old Testament only people who had seen God 'face to face' are called 'friends of God'; but the mystics who found their own selves in 'the fellowship of the Holy Spirit' called themselves God's friends because they were able to talk, and did talk, to God as a friend does. The servant begs – the child trusts – the friend consults. These are not necessarily stages in our self-confidence which we discern in prayer; but they are certainly strata of self-experience which disclose themselves to the person who prays.

1. *Our body language when we pray*

Our posture shows what we are thinking and feeling, and at the same time it influences what goes on inside us, for inwardly and outwardly, mentally and physically, we are a single Gestalt or whole. What posture do people adopt when they pray? I shall pick out three, because they are biblically based. 1. In Islam, worshippers prostrate themselves. 2. Christians fold their hands, close their eyes, kneel down. 3. The early Christians stood upright in an attitude of adoration, with raised head, open eyes and outspread arms.

1. The *Muslim* position in prayer is reminiscent of the

vassal's subservience before the absolute power of an Asiatic despot. The vassal threw himself on his face before the ruler, presenting his unprotected neck for execution or pardon, and making himself as small as possible. This age-old gesture of subservience is the expression of a religion of absolute dependence on the will of the Higher Power. But the bodily attitude implies more. The person who is praying is making himself as small as possible; he is acting out his own insignificance and assuming the position of an embryo in its mother's womb. What happens from now on is in accordance with the Lord's will. The subject's own will has been withdrawn into an embryonic condition.

But this attitude in prayer is by no means just a political gesture. In the Old Testament people who are overcome by the fathomless divine power 'fall on their faces' before it, in fear and terror. So it was with Abraham (Gen. 17.3, 17), Joshua (Josh. 7.6), Daniel (Dan. 8.17), Moses and Aaron (Lev. 16.22), and so it was with the whole people of Israel: they fell on their faces 'before the Lord' (I Kings 18.39). The New Testament tells us that Jesus 'fell on his face' in Gethsemane (Matt. 26.39) because God was 'far off' (Mark 14.41). His disciples 'fell on their faces' before Jesus when he was 'transfigured' on the mountain of God (Matt. 17.2, 6). Both God's deadly remoteness and his glorious proximity overwhelm people with unendurable terror. That is why they make themselves so small, submit themselves unconditionally, and surrender themselves completely. It is only the grace of the Almighty that gives them life.

2. The *Christian* posture in prayer in the Western church may also have developed out of gestures of political subservience in Germanic culture, although we may presume that Roman culture put a stronger impress on the church in Western Europe, and the hierarchical church evoked its own gestures of subservience.

What are we doing when we kneel down to pray, fold our hands, lower our heads and close our eyes? We are withdrawing into ourselves, assuming an attitude of contrition, and are crouched down as we are when we are doubled up

in pain. We are acting out our helplessness, our unworthiness
and our humility. We are making ourselves smaller than we
are, and seem to be sheltering from the sublime majesty of
God and his representatives on earth. Subjects were never
permitted to look their ruler in the eye. When the ruler
arrived, his subjects had to cast down their eyes so that the
potentate might remain unrecognized. Folding the hands
shows that they are unarmed, and incapable of a sudden
attack. The folded hands grasp each other; they are in firm
control of one another, so to speak. To bend the knee is a
sign of homage and an expression of profound humility. To
be 'weak at the knees', so that one is forced to sink down
before the supreme power of the Almighty, is a demon-
stration of one's own powerlessness.

In the biblical traditions, to kneel down is a way of showing that the body is sinking to the ground while the spirit
rises adoringly to God: 'O come, let us worship and bow
down, let us kneel before the Lord, our Maker!' (Ps. 95.6).
The same gesture is used into illustrate the promise of
Christ's universal lordship: 'At the name of Jesus every knee
shall bow' (Phil. 2.10). But to see people at prayer who have
crawled into themselves and are bowed down is to be
reminded of the image of the sinner used by Augustine and
Luther: 'The human being bent in upon himself' (*homo
incurvatus in se*). That person looks anything but redeemed.
Anyone who is so bent in on himself can't breathe freely. He
looks as if he is a burden to himself. What is being demonstrated here is an oppressive religion of inwardness. The
senses are closed. The human being seeks God in solitariness,
in his or her own inward being, in the heart or soul.

3. We see a completely different way of praying among
the *adoring early Christian figures* depicted in the catacombs
in Rome and Naples. They are standing upright, heads raised
and eyes open. Their arms are stretched above their heads,
their hands open, palms upwards. It is the attitude of a great
expectation and loving readiness to receive and embrace. The
people who in this posture open themselves for God are free
men and women. That is why they are standing upright and

looking up with heads held high and eyes open. They are growing beyond themselves, as it were – growing tall. The raised arms expand the chest so that the person can breathe. To stand upright is the starting point for movements in space, and invites the person to walk, stride and dance. The person who prays in this position is praying especially for the coming of the Holy Spirit: 'Come, Creator Spirit . . .' It is the attitude of Orthodox priests at the *epiklesis*. So it is not by chance that the Pentecostal movement has adopted this bodily position, and demonstrates it.

I would assume that this was the way Jesus stood in front of the disciples on the mountain where he was 'transfigured', for 'his face shone like the sun' (Matt. 17.2). It will also be the stance of people who are filled with messianic faith, and who in the uncertainties about the world's future wait for the coming of the Redeemer: 'Look up and raise your heads, because your redemption is drawing near' (Luke 21.28).

People look to the future with open eyes if for them praying means being awake, *watching*: watching in a world where so many people are suffering from nuclear and ecological numbing, out of fear of possible – or possibly inevitable – havoc.

The adoring posture of the early Christians shows the Christian faith as 'the religion of freedom', demonstrating this in a way we can enter into and feel with our senses. It is because this is a religion of freedom that in the catacombs we find a striking number of women in this posture, which expresses grandeur and self-respect, not humility. The upright stance before God is the most astonishing thing, and quite unparalleled. God is no longer feared as a superpower, and no longer exalted as the Lord of heaven by way of the worshipper's self-humiliation. Here God is like the sun that rises and shines on those who stand up to welcome it, or like the rain which the parched land receives, and which makes everything green and fertile (Matt. 5.25). To say the same thing without images; here God is Yahweh's *ruach*, the breath of life which confers life, and the wisdom of love for life. People who pray like this are laying themselves open to the wind of the Holy Spirit, and are driven by the Spirit. That is incomparable freedom before God, with God, and above all *in* God.

When we look at these three attitudes of prayer one after another, in the sequence presented here, and if we enter into each of them in our own person, we become aware of a movement that seems precisely tailored to many of the stories about Jesus in the Gospels, and is typical of them. People come to Jesus humiliated, bent down, crippled. They 'fall on their faces' in front of him and ask him for healing. And Jesus raises them up. They open themselves. They straighten their backs. They no longer look up to other people out of their misery. They look them straight in the eye. They can see again. They can walk again. They can love their lives again. They laugh and rejoice and praise the God of Israel (Matt. 15.30f.). The 'raising up' of the crippled woman is a prime example (Luke 13.10–17): 'And he laid his hands upon her, and immediately she was made straight, and praised God.' In the power she receives from Jesus, she gets up by herself and praises God in her own words.

If we begin to pray in one of life's defeats, cast down by deep disappointment or abysmal grief, it is good to begin with the first posture, and to fall on our face, roll ourselves into a ball like a child in the womb, cover our face with our hands and weep, so that the pain and anger can flow out of us. After that we rise to our knees, examining our hearts as we implore God to be near us. But healing only begins when we stand up completely, breathe deeply, raise our hands above our head, and experience with open eyes the coming of the life-giving Spirit.

These three postures can be practised when we are by ourselves, or together with close friends. They can be danced to meditative music, or painted. We can accompany them with our own voices, with sighs, prayers and rejoicing. In changing over from one posture to another it is important to listen to the language of our own bodies and to tune into it. We can also say aloud the first three petitions of the Lord's prayer in these three different positions. We shall then feel how differently the petitions are interpreted through the different postures. Isn't the adoring posture the body language that interprets them best?

> Thou hast turned for me my mourning into a round dance;
> thou hast loosed my sackcloth
> and girded me with gladness,
> that my soul may praise thee and not be silent
>
> (Ps. 30.11f.).

In 'round dances' we can dance shared experiences of God. To dance before the gods, in order to give them pleasure and to find pleasure in the gods oneself, is general practice in all cultic religions. We can still see this today from the temple dancers in India and the danced demonstrations in Africa. Israel, too, danced its experiences of God: 'Then Miriam the prophetess . . . took a tambourine in her hand and all the women went out after her with tambourines in round dances' (Ex. 15.20). But the people also danced round the Golden Calf, until Moses destroyed this image of power (Ex. 32.19). Jeremiah makes God call out in the messianic era of salvation: 'You shall take your tambourines and go forth to the dance of the merrymakers . . . Then shall the maidens rejoice in the round dance' (Jer. 31.4, 13). God is praised 'with tambourine and dancing' (Ps. 150.4). In the shared round dance the Lord's name is praised. Ever since the early Middle Ages, the church's prayer has certainly still been sung, but it is no longer danced; and this is an impoverishment of body language. How can the body be a 'temple of the Holy Spirit' if it is frozen into rigidity and is not permitted to move any more? People who are moved by God's Spirit move themselves, and people who experience grace move gracefully.

2. Coming awake and praying

Modern men and women often think that praying is something peculiar, and that in order to pray one must have a special religious aptitude. The person who goes to church is going there to pray. It is only behind monastery walls that prayer is unceasing. But modern men and women help themselves by *working*. That is why German calls the pain of grief 'the work of grief' (*Trauerarbeit*) and the experience of guilt 'mastering the past' (*Vergangenheitsbewältigung*), while self-knowledge is known as 'working on oneself' or 'self-realization'. For modern people, prayer sounds too passive. And men often think of it as 'something for the women'.

But this modern impression is quite wrong. There is nothing specially religious about praying. It is something generally and essentially human. In fact praying isn't even just something human: the whole creation prays without ceasing in the breath of the Spirit.

A sigh goes through the world

When people are seized by God's Spirit and begin to long for the redemption of this unredeemed world, they become sensitively aware, with freshly awakened senses, that this longing fills all the living who want to live and nevertheless have to die. This is the big surprise which Paul describes in his Letter to the Romans (8.19ff.); 'All who are led by the Spirit of God are children of God', he had said earlier (8.14), and we think: 'Great for us!' But then he sets this human experience of the Spirit in the context of a universal cosmic expectation: 'The creation waits with fearful longing for the revealing of the children of God . . . because the creation itself desires to be set free from its bondage to decay and obtain the glorious liberty of the children of God' (8.19, 21). Together with the whole of creation, 'fearful' because of evanescent time and the destiny of death, we long for the redemption of the body. The torments of death and the yearning for life make all earthly creatures sigh and groan, and join in our sighing and groaning. For where these sighs and groans are heard there is still hope for redemption. Where everything in and around us is struck dumb, hope dies too. Sighs and groans are hope's signs of life, in opposition to death. That is why, according to Rom. 8.26, God's Spirit, the life-giver, also intercedes for us 'with sighs too deep to utter' when we ourselves feel we can't go on, and are struck dumb. But this means nothing other than that God himself suffers in his creation and with his creation, and sustains it through his sym-pathetic suffering and sighing patience, until the day of redemption dawns and his glory is revealed in all creatures, so that there is no further need to remember 'this time of suffering'.

So when in the Spirit who is the life-giver we human beings begin to complain of death and to weep for our dead, we shall wake up and hear how the earth weeps, and how all its creatures groan and cry.

When we come awake in God's Spirit, we also participate in God's sufferings in this world and with this world, and wait for the future of his redemption. In this sense praying simply means doing what the earth with all its living things does, and doing what God himself does in the world through his Spirit. It is not praying any more that is the singular thing, because it singles out silent human beings from the crying and groaning earth. Not to pray any more means not to come awake, but to be numbed by God's absence.

The world is full of praise

There would be no fear of death if there were no delight in life, and there would be no sighing in the world if there were no love for life there. Indeed the stronger the delight in life, the deeper the fear of death, and the more passionate the love for life, the louder the sighs and groans. The sighs and the song of praise are not contradictions. They reinforce each other mutually. The pain of death is simply the negative, reverse side of the positive love for life.

The world is full of praise, for God is in this world. God is not far off, in the Beyond, but is himself the life in the world. Israel expressed this by saying that God's Spirit, God's Wisdom and God's presence fill everything created in such a way that all things live from God and have their existence and continuance in God. 'The Spirit of the Lord fills the world' (Wisdom 1.7). His Wisdom 'reaches from one end of the earth to the other in goodness' (Wisdom 8.1). 'God's immortal spirit is in all things' (Wisdom 12.1). But one day 'the whole earth will be full of his glory', as Isaiah 'saw' in his call vision (Isa. 6.3). So nothing is so far from God that it does not hold God 'within itself', as Aquinas said, and God is so close to all things that, together with human beings, in him 'they live, move and have their being' (Acts 17.28). How do we perceive this? All created things praise, love, glorify and adore God by rejoicing over their existence before him, and by enjoying their life in God. 'All thy works give thanks to thee' (Ps. 145.10). 'The field exults and everything in it. All the trees of the wood sing for joy' (Ps. 96.12). 'The heavens are telling the glory of God', says Psalm 19, and Job 26 is the record of a wonderful hymn of creation.

It is only for modern men and women that the world has become dumb, for it has now come to be seen merely as material for research and technology. The modern world for its part has led to what Rachel Carson called 'the silent spring', and has turned the song of praise of living creation into the stillness of the dead and ravaged world. But the world is not mute. All creatures speak, even if human beings can no longer hear them. All creatures are aflame with the present glory of the Lord, and reflect his glory in a thousand different mirrors, but 'we are blind, we have no eyes' said Calvin, as did Francis of Assisi.

People who thank God every morning for the new day in their lives, people who praise God through their delight in existence and glorify him through their love for life, are not doing something singular. They are only doing what all creatures do, universally and unceasingly, each in its own way. With the lives they live these people are joining in with cosmic resonance of God's goodness and beauty. To pray like this means to wake up out of the mute world of modernity and turn back to the cosmic solidarity of all created being.

Praying means coming awake. So praying also means *awakening the senses.*

> Awake, my heart, and sing
> the Maker of all things,

wrote Paul Gerhardt, and:

> What the great God so greatly does
> awakens all my senses.

People used to call this 'nature mysticism'. Nowadays the phrase is 'creation spirituality'. If this is not to get stuck at the level of religious poetry, we must develop a new theological understanding of nature which will teach us to read nature – from matter to human beings – as God's sign language, so that we may learn to hear and see, taste and feel God in all things and all things in God. As creation, nature is more than an information system which we make out so as to master and reproduce it. The genetic code and our cultural code point beyond themselves to God's sign language, just as this sign language can gather up the genetic and cultural codes so that they take on a new quality.

The laughter of the universe is God's delight

When in the company of all other created beings we praise God for our existence, and when we glorify him through our lives, we are praising his goodness as Creator and his marvellous patience with us. He leaves us time and gives us living space. But he also gives us an experience of God which takes us further than that: the knowledge of the raising of Jesus Christ from the dead, and his transfiguration in the coming glory of God. It is the experience of 'the power of the resurrection' out of which we ourselves are born again to a living hope. This is the overture to the transformation of this temporal creation into the eternal creation, and this mortal life into eternal life. In this overture, all the harmonies and melodies of the future symphony of the world in God are already sounded. From it a supernatural joy springs up which overcomes the sighs, and gathers into itself the songs of praise of this creation. The joy is not restricted to the

Easter faith, for this human Easter faith is set in cosmic dimensions.

Adoration in 'wonder, love and praise' is outdone yet again by the *'Easter laughter'*. This was originally a medieval custom, a way of translating the Easter joy into earthly pleasures too. The congregation was to be made to laugh through jokes and fun. We can still hear this laughter echoing in the words and tunes of Easter hymns. The Easter laughter springs from the completely unexpected and totally surprising universal turning point which God initiated when he raised Jesus – the Jesus whom the powers of this world had crucified, and whom the women who followed him had buried. At first, certainly, the women and the disciples were simply shocked. But the laughter at this turn of events, which already fills the community of the risen Christ here and now, will one day ring through the whole universe, when the universe is raised and transfigured in the glory of God. What had been expected was the cosmic catastrophe, and what comes is the new creation. What had been expected was cosmic death, and what comes is eternal life. Is that not reason enough for laughter? With us prayer and laughter seem to be poles apart. But here they coincide. 'Then our mouth will be filled with laughter and our tongue with shouts of joy' (Ps. 126.2), for 'blessed are you that weep now, for you shall laugh' (Luke 6.21).

3. Wanting – willing – praying

Prayer doesn't come easily to the lips of some people, let alone spontaneously. Of course in every life there are heartfelt sighs and cries from the depths. But prayer is more than that. It is talking to God and with God, and if in the fellowship of Christ God is 'our Father', then his children will like to talk to him, always and everywhere. A child grows slowly and learns to talk to its parents; and the same is true in our relationship to God, which is the relation of a child. We pray through the Holy Spirit, and we listen to God in the Spirit, and through prayer we grow into fellowship with God. Faith deepens prayer, and prayer strengthens faith, until we reach the point of 'praying always and without ceasing' (Luke 18.1), whether consciously or unconsciously. Of course we shouldn't just babble on at length 'as the Gentiles do' (Matt. 6.7); but we are struck to the heart when in the Gethsemane story we hear Jesus's reproach to the disciples: 'Could you not watch with me *one hour?*' It isn't easy to pray concentratedly for a longish time, let alone 'one hour' in the day, without letting one's thoughts stray. But prayer and meditation have this in common: they can only be learnt by hard, concentrated practice. So we must practise praying, like to pray, and feel the spiritual strengthening and comfort we receive in prayer. Christians who have to get through a huge daily agenda are often the very ones who spend a very long time in sustained prayer.

The psalms in the Old Testament can be a good school of prayer, and so can the Lord's Prayer and the church's hymnbook, because they embody so much, and have so much to tell us, about the loss of God, the experience of God, and the wisdom of God. We need this tradition in order to find our own language in prayer, and not to be reduced to silence.

And if a man in torment is struck dumb,
yet did a god give words to tell my suffering (Goethe).

As specifically as possible

What must we bring with us when we pray? We are talking now about prayers of request. If we take our bearings from the stories about Jesus in the Gospels, we see that there are two necessary preconditions if the request is to be heard: 1. *firm faith*, in the sense that we trust God with all our heart and all our soul and all our strength, since 'All things are possible with God'; 2. *a strong will* that what we have prayed for should really happen. 'Your faith has made you well', said Jesus to 'the woman with an issue of blood', who touches his garment, being sure that if she does so she will be healed (Mark 5.34). 'Be it done for you as you desire', he says to the Canaanite woman who begs him to heal her daughter (Matt. 15.28). We must bring faith to prayer, and we must know exactly what we want. What we want we must want under all circumstances.

Praying begins with *wishing*. We get an idea, we have a dream, we see a vision in front of us. Nothing lends more vitality than a creative idea. It gives us hope and points us towards a greater future. Our life takes on meaning, and what we do acquires an orientation. Why is there so much despair and apathy about? Because we have betrayed our dreams and lost our hopes. Because we are afraid of being disappointed we write off our hopes so quickly, and don't dare to do things. 'Blessed is he who expects nothing, for he will not be disappointed,' we say. This attitude often leads us to make a cunning deal with providence: I always expect the worst. If it doesn't happen, great! If it does – well, at least I was right. But hope wants whatever I am beginning to be successful, and have a happy end. The person who really expects and hopes for something is not in love with failure. If we really want something, we have to want it with all our hearts and all our souls and all our strength. It is better to come to grief with our great wishes than not to have them, and to be successful as a result.

The same can be said about what we *will*. Praying begins with what we really *will*, with all our hearts and all our souls and all our strength. Here too we are often gnawed by doubts about the things our will is set on. 'It's impossible', we say, and don't trust ourselves to do it: 'I can't!' By saying this we are already anticipating in our innermost souls the possible setbacks, and are getting in the way of our own 'willing'. So as not to be completely disappointed, we only 'will' half-heartedly, our hearts are not in it, and we do not invest all our energies. But how should that 'be done for as we desire' (Matt. 15.28) if we are not clear ourselves about what we really do desire, and whether we actually desire it at all? Let us put ourselves for a moment in the position of the one who is supposed to be responding to our wanting, will-ing and praying. Does he hear a clear wish, a specific will and a real, solid request? Are we trusting him to hear our requests with complete trust? Faith means wanting and willing some-thing with all our hearts.

As unreservedly as we can

Faith like this must be brought to prayer, or must be developed in prayer. People who don't love and trust God with their whole heart (Deut. 6.5) don't truly pray either. So we have to banish every germ of resignation from our minds. We have to conquer our apprehension that what we wish and pray for might perhaps not happen after all. It is not trusting God if we ask for something, but immediately leave it to him not to answer our request. That sounds as if we were saying: 'Yes, we are asking, but we don't much care whether what we ask is granted or not.' If we bring our wish-ing and willing to God in prayer, we are trusting ourselves to God completely, and expecting everything of him. According to the stories in the Bible, people who came to Jesus asking something had a clear picture in their minds of what they desired and willed, and they came to him with unreserved trust. So when we pray, let us make our wishes and requests as clear and specific as we possibly can. Let us banish every-thing that is hazy and equivocal; don't let us keep our options open! And let us trust ourselves to God with a whole and undivided heart, and without resignation: 'All things are possible with God!'

There is a build-up in prayer. This is the transition from *prayer* to meditation, and from *meditation* to the silent *sub-mergence* in God. We begin with our wants and requests. We take up our thinking and thanking. These are the gifts of grace for which we ask and give thanks. But then we perceive the gracious hand of God out of whose fullness we receive and take, and we grasp these open hands of the life-giving God, so to speak. From these open hands of God we will be led to the open heart or 'womb' of God, in which we are

eternally in safe keeping. These images are a way of describing the road that leads from asking in God to life in God.
Finally, we no longer love God just because of his gifts of
grace, which make life endurable and good. Then we no
longer love God either just because of his wonderful
presence, which surrounds us from every side. Then we begin
to love God for his own sake and are happy in a kind of
selfless contemplation of his beauty. In this *adoration* we fall
silent, because we forget ourselves. The silent submergence of
the heart in God does not do away with the other stages in
prayer. The mystic way which we have described here is not
an outward journey with no return. On the contrary, it
means turning into ourselves so that we can start on a new
outward journey, and an immersion in the mystery of life so
that it may be more vital. So it is good in prayer to fall silent
between the remembering and the thanking and the wanting
and the requesting, so that as we become still we may sense
the presence of God in the eternal moment.

In the name of Jesus

Perhaps our prayers often remain so general and resigned
because we only call on God without being clear in our own
minds who God is. Then it is a help to name *the name of
Jesus*, to call on God in his name, and to make our requests
for his sake. With Jesus, we have in our mind's eye a specific
human figure. This makes it clear to us what we can pray and
how; for Jesus makes us aware of who God is. When we look
at Jesus's person and message, we realize what we can ask
for, and what we can't. He is the visible likeness of the
invisible God. That is why he was rightly called the Son of
God, and God's Word made flesh. To see Jesus is to see God.
The way Jesus listens and acts is the way God listens and
acts. The One Jesus called 'Abba, my beloved Father' is, for
Jesus's sake and in fellowship with him, our Father too.
'Abba' is a primal word of undivided childlike trust. So we
can also translate it as 'mother'. We must see what form of
address in prayer best expresses our undivided primal trust.

I feel Jesus's nearness most strongly in addressing God as Abba. That is why we pray the Lord's prayer in the fellowship of Jesus. Later prayer formularies in the church then addressed prayers 'through Christ to the Father'. Just as through Jesus God the Father became our Father too, so through Jesus we talk to God our Father. In order to make that clear, it is useful to pray 'Our Father who art in Christ.' When we say 'our Father in heaven', it is because we are thinking of God in the kingdom of his boundless possibilities; but we also feel a distance which was not present in Jesus's Abba prayer. 'Our Father in Christ' brings God down to earth from heaven, so to speak. However we use it, it is only with the name of Jesus that our prayers become concrete, and that trust enters into our prayer.

4. *Living with unheard prayers is called 'watching'*

How can we go on living with unanswered prayers and still keep our trust in God? How can we exist when God is silent? Then suffering from God begins, with the unanswerable and inexorable question: My God, why? And suffering from our own unfulfilled lives begins also: 'Why me?' or 'Why not me?' Many people then give up and stop praying altogether, because it hasn't helped anyway. Many people give up believing in God, or rebel against this God who leaves us in the lurch when we need him. 'Curse God and die', Job's atheistic wife advised him, as he sat on the ashes of his life and contended with God. When Jesus's prayer in Gethsemane was not heard, his disciples fell into a deep sleep. That, too, is a natural reaction to absolute desolation.

If our prayers are not heard, and we feel only soundless silence round about us, it is good to think of Gethsemane, and to enter in spirit into Jesus's passionate prayer to his heavenly Father, and into his God-forsakenness. He was not spared the cup of forsakenness for whose passing he had so implored. Not his will was done but God's, the will he did not want. Any of us who find again our own god-forsakenness in the forsakenness of the Jesus who prayed without an answer, enter into an experience of God which the Christian mystics later called 'the dark night of the soul'. We would give up, or become inwardly numbed, or as if turned to stone, were we not together with Jesus to acquire the power to 'watch' in this 'night of God'. Watching means being aware, open-eyed and with fully stretched senses, of the reality of this eclipse of God. The New Testament does not simply say 'pray!' We are told again and again to 'watch and pray'. We learn this watching in fellowship with Jesus, when God is far away from us. It is a watching and waiting in the Holy Spirit, who is beside us and intercedes for us when we lose sight of God and when the last spark of faith in us dies out. The watching Christ in Gethsemane shows us this way of being open for God's reality in God's absence. Watching in tense expectation is the strongest form of prayer, because it is a great human answer to God's hiddenness. We watch for God.

'Be sober, be vigilant': this is what the New Testament expects of Christians. They are supposed to keep watch in a sleeping, drunken and dreaming world. What do we perceive, when we live with senses that are open to receive and at full stretch? We perceive the dangers threatening the world, and the tribulations hanging over its self-assured and despairing people. But we watch, too, because we are watching for God's coming. 'Blessed are those whom the Lord shall find watching when he comes' (Luke 12.37). Waiting puts great expectancy into our praying, and by so doing makes it messianic. Watching goes beyond the praying and beyond the falling silent, because it makes our whole life an animated and awakened life in tense expectation of God's coming into this world.

5. The sustaining network of intercession

It is actually astonishing that I can pray not just for myself but for other people, too, and that other people can pray not only for themselves but for me as well. These intercessions bring us into a great, often world-wide fellowship of the

Spirit. To know that this fellowship is there, and intercedes for me when I fall silent, gives me a powerful feeling of safe keeping. In this intercessory dimension, praying doesn't make us solitary; it overcomes our lonelinesses. People who have a hard time ahead of them and know that others are praying for them know that they are sustained, and they don't give up. Human life becomes living when people are there for each other; and in the same way, life in the Spirit becomes a living life because people pray for each other, and bring one another reciprocally to God.

Intercession cannot remain general. It has to be specific. But it can only be specific if we have as much background knowledge as possible, and inform ourselves. 'Informed prayer' is therefore a convincing point in the programme for the *Women's World Day of Prayer*, which has existed ever since 1887 and which has become a world-wide ecumenical movement. Each year, on the first Friday in March,

> women all over the world support each other in their hopes and fears, their joys and anxieties, the possibilities open to them and their needs. Through the World Day of Prayer women all over the world are encouraged to raise their sights to include the whole world, and no longer to live in isolation; to take upon themselves the burden of other people and to pray with them and for them; to become conscious of their gifts and to put them to use in the service of the community. Through the World Day of Prayer, women confirm that prayer and action cannot be separated, and that both have an influence in the world which cannot be estimated' (*Ein Freitag im März*, ed. A. Schmidt-Biesalski, Weltgebetshandbuch, 1982).

Informed prayer for other people leads us to share in the fortunes of other people, suffer with them and rejoice with them. Because people's lives are never merely inward or spiritual, informed intercession leads inescapably to social, political and economic prayer for others who are humiliated, hungry and oppressed. After all, the Lord's Prayer already puts 'our daily bread' first when it turns to human affairs.

Today, all over the world, the Women's World Day of Prayer has become an eminently political matter, no less than the *Political Night Prayers* which began in Cologne in Germany, and the world-wide *prayers for peace*.

Depending on the possibilities and powers available, informed prayer is followed essentially by *'praying action'*. In many countries the Women's World Day of Prayer has triggered off unexpected initiatives and activities. The prayers for peace held on Monday evenings in the Protestant churches in Leipzig are another good example of informed prayer and its results. These prayers were a leftover from the massive peace movement at the beginning of the 1980s, when people in West and East Germany demonstrated against the introduction of Cruise missiles. For ten long years, some very small, politically quite insignificant groups met in Leipzig to pray for peace. Then came the unforgettable peace demonstrations of 1989, which took 300,000 people on to the streets. It was the Monday evening prayers for peace which first sparked off the demonstrations and the commitment to non-violence. Against 'prayers and candles' the full martial force of the state power of East Germany was helpless. These Leipzig prayers for peace and peace demonstrations brought down the Berlin wall, and because they were non-violent they may be considered the first successful revolution in Germany.

A Prayer

God, creator of heaven and earth,
it is time for you to come,
for our time is running out
and our world is passing away.
You gave us life in peace, one with another,
and we have ruined it in mutual conflict.
You made your creation in harmony and equilibrium.
We want progress, and are destroying ourselves.
Come Creator of all things,
renew the face of the earth.

Come, Lord Jesus,
our brother on our way.
You came to seek
that which was lost.
You have come to us and have found us.
Take us with you on your way.
We hope for your kingdom
as we hope for peace.
Come, Lord Jesus, come soon.

Come, Spirit of life,
flood us with your light,
interpenetrate us with your love.
Awaken our powers through your energies
and in your presence let us be wholly there.
Come, Holy Spirit.

God, Father, Son and Holy Spirit,
triune God,
unite with yourself your torn and divided world,
and let us all be one in you,
one with your whole creation,
which praises and glorifies you
and in you is happy.
Amen.

Suggestions for Further Reading

H. Berkhof, *The Doctrine of the Holy Spirit, The Warfield Lectures 1963–64*, John Knox Press 1964 and Epworth Press 1965

J.V. Taylor, *The Go-Between God*, SCM Press 1972

Y. Congar, *I Believe in the Holy Spirit*, Geoffrey Chapman 1983

J. Sobrino, *Spirituality of Liberation*, Orbis Books 1988

S.J. Land, *Pentecostal Spirituality. A Passion for the Kingdom*, Sheffield Academic Press 1993

D. Yonggi, *Patterns of Prayer*, Seoul 1993

S.E. Saliers, *Worship as Theology. Foretaste of Glory Divine*, Abingdon Press 1994

M. Welker, *God the Spirit*, Fortress Press 1994

G. Müller-Fahrenholz, *God's Spirit Transforming a World in Crisis*, World Council of Churches 1995

R.H. Schuller, *Prayer: My Soul's Adventure with God. A Spiritual Biography*, Abingdon Press 1996

C.H. Pinnock, *Flame of Love. A Theology of the Holy Spirit*, Intervarsity Press USA 1996

Index of Names